Royal Style Wars

CRESCENT BOOKS
New York

Royal Style Wars

LESLEY EBBETTS

This 1990 edition is published by Crescent Books
Distributed by Crown Publishers, Inc.

Copyright © Brian Trodd Publishing House Limited 1988,
1990

ISBN 0-517-69239-2

h g f e d c b

Printed in Hong Kong

On the balcony of Buckingham
Palace after Trooping the
Colour in July 1987.
The Princess of Wales is in a
cream silk gaberdine suit by
Victor Edelstein and a Philip
Somerville hat in cream raw silk
with bow made from the fabric
of the suit.
The Duchess of York is wearing
a printed silk satin pleated dress
by Lindka Cierach with a semi-
fitted linen jacket and matching
linen belt. Her hat is by Freddie
Fox. Both outfits were originally
designed for Ascot.

Contents

The Duchess of York on tour in Mauritius in the autumn of 1987 wearing a navy and white dress by Lindka Cierach and a magnificent navy straw hat.
The hat is decorated with pale pink silk roses and glossy, deep green preserved rhododendron leaves, the stems of which are twisted to make a natural headband. The Duchess is carrying a bouquet of the Mauritian national flower.

The Princess of Wales on a stop-over in Fiji on the way from Australia in autumn 1985.
She is in an outfit of pure silk, coffee and cream, and wearing a hat by Marina Killery.
Her necklace was a gift from Prince Charles after the birth of Prince William.

1 *Introduction*

When on Wednesday 23 July, 1986, Sarah Ferguson walked down the aisle of Westminster Abbey on the arm of—unquestionably—the most charismatic of the Royal brothers Windsor, she not only took on a new husband and all the joys and responsibilities of being married to Prince Andrew, now Duke of York, Earl of Inverness, Baron of Killyleagh, but also acquired some fierce public scrutiny.

The public, while devoted to the Royal Family, was nevertheless used to an almost daily diet of Royal fashion facts, figures and criticism of her great and long-standing friend Diana, Princess of Wales. Even on this happy day the Royal-watchers, to give them their polite name, were already wondering how the slender, elegant and very stylish Princess of Wales would dress so as not to cause comment. Would she underplay her unrivalled dress sense in order not to outshine the new Duchess of York? The press had created a rivalry, albeit false, between the two Royal ladies from almost the moment the engagement was announced between Andrew and Sarah.

Unable to resist the temptation to set them fashionably one against the other, the press made the clothes worn by these two highly attractive Royals extremely visible. Major newspapers, TV networks and magazines the world over reported, and judged, their wardrobes and their style with as much attention as their official and, in some cases unofficial, engagements.

Unintentionally they had, through their popularity, become the centre of a sartorial competition, the mythical Royal Style Wars.

For Sarah particularly, this was a harsh time but, seemingly unfussed, she kept her head and her own particular style, love it or hate it, throughout her first years of marriage in the public eye.

Both women grew in stature during this time, with the Princess of Wales continuing to gracefully represent British fashion by wearing it

Above:
Sarah Ferguson in March 1986 leaving the office of B.C.K. Graphic Arts, a publishing firm in Mayfair, where she worked. The previous day her engagement to Prince Andrew had been announced. She is wearing a cashmere cardigan by Ralph Lauren.

Below.
The New Face in the Crowd.
Prince Andrew and Sarah
Ferguson at Ascot in June 1986,
shortly before their wedding.

Left:
Young friends together at
polo in Windsor in the summer
of 1982.
Princess Diana was pregnant
with William and is wearing a
polka dot design maternity
dress by Catherine Walker.

so extensively. For she is, by any standard, our brightest star, be it Royal or show business. Since her first faltering steps as a fresh-faced fiancee of Prince Charles and her entry into the public glare in March 1981, she has perfectly dressed the part of the wife of the heir to the throne. She has done this while setting astonishing new precedents in Royal dress for one so young.

No previous Royal had invited help from outside the Royal circle. No Royal had taken so instantly to fashion trends, almost making them her own. No Royal before had used the advice of so many designers; Royals chose dressmakers and couturiers and then stayed loyal to one, or maybe two. No previous Royal had bought off-the-peg clothes for official tours and engagements.

Princess Diana's choice of clothes has brought a new awareness of British designer talent to a previously unfashion-conscious public. Her influence, and that of the Duchess of York, is enormous. Social history will one day show how the fixation with Royal fashion became important for the industry and created an interest worldwide in British trends. For while it may have gone unheeded in the more exclusive fashion capitals, unless of course an overseas tour took the Royal ladies within their shores, the interest in Royal fashion produced a wealth of homemade critics and amateur pundits.

Both Diana and Sarah created this haute couture influence while insisting that they were not really interested in fashion. The truth, surely,is that until they inadvertently created this mass interest in fashion, clothes were something the majority of the British did not care about. Trends—particularly of the excellence the Princess of Wales invests in—and spending money on top designers, were for the few and considered almost immoral. The British woman has never believed in spending a great deal on clothes. Her home, her kitchen maybe, but not her wardrobe. Her European counterpart would not think twice about such an investment. The Princess, and now the Duchess, have made British women reconsider.

Below:
In June 1981 Lady Diana Spencer attended the wedding of Nicholas Soames wearing a dress of red spotted silk with blue and green stars by Neil and Fortescue.
The red hat with upturned brim and huge bow was designed by John Boyd.
Later the hat was sent back to be re-trimmed in green and was worn for the first day of a tour of Wales in November of the same year.

Left:
Both Diana and Sarah attended a friend's wedding shortly before they were married themselves.
At the wedding of Carolyn Beckwith-Smith in July 1986, Sarah Ferguson chose a white silk faconne jacket over a green and white printed faconne dress by Lindka Cierach.
Her matching green hat was by Freddie Fox.

There is, and always has been, a world of difference between wearing clothes that suit the job and wearing fashion to emphasise a time. In the nature of their duties, the Princess and the Duchess, unlike other women, have to do both.

Royal style rules have previously decreed that one must dress suitably, however dull, and must definitely not draw attention to oneself unnecessarily. The exception is the use of brightly coloured fabrics so as to help visibility in a crowd.

Diana and Sarah have changed all that. They both knew how to dress inconspicuously in their private lives, in clothes that suited them and their set. But given the job in the public eye, centre stage, to perform their Royal duties, the temptation was clearly too inviting. They both turned to the top designers, the trendiest, the most prolific of the day, to create looks for them.

The results have been staggering. Diana particularly has always bravely gone where few earlier Royals would have dared to tread. The way she has combined diplomacy, style and suitability, while remaining beautifully dressed by so many of her favourite British designers, has turned her into a star.

The Duchess is now following that lead. As an old friend of Diana's and in the position of Duchess of York, it was only right that she should have as much fun with clothes as the job allows.

It was clear from the start that Sarah was a totally different personality from the 'shy Di' image the Princess of Wales had when she first married. Sarah has a confidence which enables her to make everyone she meets feel at ease. She is bolder. She has a terrific sense of fun and almost refuses to take fashion seriously, except for accepting that dealing with designers is now part of the job. She fits them into her busy schedule, which she has already explained takes up twenty-five hours of a twenty-four hour day. Any woman running

two careers will know what that means! Her career in publishing in the London office of the Swiss firm, BCK Graphic Arts, was important to her. She is clearly very talented.

Now she is an author in her own right with two children's books about a helicopter called Budgie and its adventures published by Simon and Schuster, with the promise of more to follow. The Duchess is well informed on flying, being the first female member of the Royal Family to hold a pilot's licence.

Whether she knew it or not, she had already begun to set trends. Her skirt, at that time, was considerably longer than most young girls were wearing—and had an instant impact. The mid-calf length was simply not new any more.

The Princess of Wales, at the time of her own engagement photo call, stepped out arm-in-arm with Prince Charles. She was wearing an off-the-peg Cojana suit from Harrods, very conventional and suitable. But it was her shoes that everyone noticed, not her suit. They were flat, and started a trend that only abated in 1987.

The Princess, then Lady Diana, began to give all kinds of old fashions an elegance, even flat shoes!

Her mother, who had her clothes made at Bellville Sassoon (behind Harrods), naturally took her newly-engaged daughter to have her engagement wardrobe personally made by David Sassoon. David

Right:
Prince Andrew and Sarah Ferguson on the lawn of Buckingham Palace on the day of their engagement announcement.
Sarah chose a navy wool crepe, double-breasted jacket with pewter buttons on the sleeve. The jacket was short and boxy and belted in black leather with a silver buckle.
Her extra long skirt was worn with a purple silk vest. Designed by Alistair Blair, the outfit was the first to be created for the bride-to-be and was made in only 24 hours.

Above:
A beautiful ring on beautiful hands.
Prince Andrew and Sarah Ferguson on the announcement of their engagement in March 1986 show to the world the stunning ring which the Prince himself helped design.
Created from 10 diamonds and a large ruby set in yellow and white gold, the ring was bought from the Royal Jewellers, Garrard

Far right:
A shy young Lady Diana Spencer on the announcement of her engagement in February 1981.
Walking with her husband-to-be from Buckingham Palace to the lawn, Diana wears a sapphire blue silk suit with scallop edges and a white silk blouse with blue bird motif.
The outfit was made by the London fashion house Cojana and was bought from Harrods.

Right:
Celebrating their marriage with the thousands who came to cheer them, the Duke and Duchess of York on the balcony of Buckingham Palace.

went on to create many 'first' outfits for her, including her pretty, young 'cantaloupe' silk shantung going-away dress and jacket that, with John Boyd's tricorn hat, were an instant fashion trend. The shops rapidly filled with little 'Lady Diana hats' and organza collars.

The wedding dress, a perfect combination of fantasy and romance, was made by the Emanuels, David and Elizabeth. They were leading young designers in couture, and for the rather theatrical setting of St Paul's Cathedral with its wide, grand nave, an excellent choice as Royal wedding dress designers. Their clothes are dramatic, the wearer feeling as though she has stepped back into the era of Scarlett O'Hara or perhaps the Elizabethan court.

The train alone was 25 feet long, sparkling with mother-of- pearl sequins and tiny pearls which decorated the lace. David and Elizabeth made the dress in ivory pure silk taffeta with an overlayer of pearl-encrusted lace.

Although a young girl, just twenty, Lady Diana was keen to uphold

Above:
The whole family celebrates 'The Kiss' on the balcony of Buckingham Palace after the wedding on 23 July 1986. Carrying Prince Harry, Diana looks on wearing a figure-hugging turquoise and black spot silk satin dress with the newest basque waistline made of finely pleated black satin. Her matching turn-back brimmed hat is by Kirsten Woodward.

tradition. She had something rather special as her 'something old'—the lace forming the panels of her dress was the Carrickmacross lace that once belonged to Queen Mary. The Emanuels had it dyed a slightly lighter shade in order to make a perfect match with the ivory dress. Her 'something blue' was a little blue bow which had been stitched into the waist band of the dress. The 'something borrowed' was the Spencer tiara and her mother's diamond earrings, but the little keepsake that was all of her own making was for luck. Concealed in the folds of the luxurious silk taffeta was a minute gold and diamond horseshoe. Her slippers were in silk and had a central heart motif made with nearly 150 pearls and 500 sequins by Clive Shilton. Her flowers were a rather sad reminder of the honorary Grandfather who could not be there—Mountbatten golden roses in a tumbling arrangement by Jane Packer of freesias, lily of the valley, stephanotis, white orchids and trailing ivy leaves. Another touch of history was woven into the bouquet with myrtle and veronica from bushes planted by Queen Victoria at her home, Osborne House, on the Isle of Wight.

It was truly a fairytale wedding for anyone watching on 29 July 1981. However, it was also very grand and full of historical meaning, to which the Duke and Duchess, when they married five years later almost to the day, were not tethered.

Sarah's dress was created by a previously unknown designer, Lindka Cierach, a very personal choice. Like everything that happened that day, it was exactly as Sarah planned it—beautiful and, in spite of the awe-inspiring Abbey, almost informal.

The dress took 10 weeks to make, with one dressmaker working on it constantly. It was made in rich ivory silk Duchess satin, with a fitted boned bodice dropped to below the waist and coming into a point at the front and a lower 'V' at the back. The gently curved neckline was edged with pearls, as were the sleeves at the elbow. The skirt was flat at the front, widening to the sides and full at the back. Her underskirt was finished with a silk scalloped lace flounce.

Sarah's train was a work of art. At 17½ feet long, it fell from beneath a fan-shaped bow. The beadwork on the dress and the train showed Sarah's own coat of arms—thistles attended by bees, tied with ribbon and incorporating an 'S' for Sarah. This theme was interwoven with anchors, waves and hearts on the train, with an heraldic 'A' and 'S' design. The total number of bugle beads, sequins, crystals, pearls and stones amounted to 155,000. Her veil was made of pure silk bonninet and was scalloped with embroidered hearts along the edge and punctuated with guipure lace bows. Sparkling throughout the service, the veil was covered with tiny sequins.

The personal touch of arriving like a country girl with flowers in her hair and, after the pronouncement, returning from the signing of the register as a Duchess in a regal tiara, without the flowers, was entirely Sarah's idea. It charmed everyone and gave a marvellously family atmosphere, even though it was our *Royal* family, to the whole day.

2 Into the Limelight

Current fashion comes into marked focus at a grand Royal evening engagement. They are opulent, uplifting, fun occasions whenever attended by either the Princess or the Duchess.

There is nowadays a sense of sophistication and elegance that pervades the British evening dress scene, due in no small measure to the example that Diana and Sarah have set. Dressing-up is something the Princess of Wales loves and Sarah is learning to.

Before their influence, evening dresses for the Royal Family—for the Queen, the Queen Mother, even for the Princesses Alexandra, Margaret and Anne—were aptly called 'function dresses' by the designers. However, to call Diana and Sarah's evening dresses functional would do them a great disservice. There is nothing in the least underplayed or just plain practical about the designs that they have at their disposal and, because of the steady development of British designer-talent, there is admiration and a desire to emulate their lead in this rich, regal and expensive end of the fashion scene.

Dressing-up is now *de rigeur.* It began when the Princess of Wales, then Lady Diana Spencer, wore a strapless black taffeta evening dress to her first official engagement, a recital at the Goldsmiths' Hall in aid of the Covent Garden Opera House. There was mild indignation, a small public outcry, that one in line for marriage to the heir to the throne could be so daring.

However, the fashion press applauded, recognising an independent fashion spirit. Instantly, the fashion business started to produce strapless taffeta evening dresses at any price. It was the first indication of what was to come for the young Lady Diana and an insatiable mass market. One visit to Laura Ashley, a much-loved haunt in Harriet Street, Knightsbridge, of the then unknown Diana Spencer, even now will

Above:
As patron of Birthright, the Princess of Wales attends a fashion show at Guildhall in November 1982. She chose an electric blue frilled print crepe de chine evening dress by Bruce Oldfield. The dress was unusual with an asymmetric hem and one-shouldered neckline.

Right:
*The Princess of Wales attends
a gala evening in aid of the
Order of St John at the
Barbican Arts and Conference
Centre in spring 1982.
Pregnant with Prince William
she is wearing a claret empire-
line silk taffeta dress which was
part of a complete maternity
wardrobe made for her by
Bellville Sassoon. The dress was
worn only during pregnancy.*

Above:
*The Duchess of York attending
a ball at the Royal College of
Art, Kensington, in aid of the
NSPCC in June 1987. She wears
a red-ribboned embroidered
evening gown, edged in frills
with a low waistline and huge
bow back by Yves St Laurent.*

provide proof of the strength of the Princess' leadership in fashion—the taffeta ball gown is still selling.

It wasn't, as it turned out, such a devastatingly new idea. Whether the Princess was already exercising her wit and wisdom of fashion so early in her public life is not known. However, she would not have had any disapproval from the Queen, who had had a strapless, low-cut dress of similar style made for evening wear shortly after her engagement to Prince Philip. Sarah Ferguson also decided on a strapless evening dress, from the designer who was to make her wedding dress, Lindka Cierach, in black velvet with a boned bodice draped with black lace.

Good haute couture, beautifully executed by a couturier, used to be all that previous ladies of the Royal family desired. Once

Arriving for a dinner in Edmonton during the tour of Canada in summer 1987, the Duchess of York emerges from the Royal Car in a floating silk tulle and chiffon ball gown—a work of art by Zandra Rhodes.

The Princess of Wales in a glittering, beaded evening dress by Catherine Walker being greeted as she arrives at the Reception at Claridges in London for King Hasam of Morocco in 1987.

Above:
First seen during the Australian tour in 1983 the Princess of Wales has worn this, perhaps her most glamorous dress ever, on several occasions. It is a breathtakingly stylish and slim-fitting sequinned evening gown by the Japanese designer Hachi.

21

Below:
Below:
The Duchess of York arrives at the Royal Opera House, Covent Garden for a performance of 'Fanfare for Elizabeth' in celebration of the Queen's 60th birthday. She wears a dress by Alistair Blair in three colours of duchess satin—ivory, black and blue. Fitted into the waist, it has long sleeves, a large off-the-shoulder cuff collar and trimmings of rhinestone buttons on the cuffs.

Below, right:
For a premiere of 'Back to the Future' in aid of the Prince's Trust at the Empire, Leicester Square, December 1985, the Princess wears a rich panne velvet plunge-backed dress designed by Catherine Walker.

those couturiers were found, and their discretion obtained, previous Royal ladies never felt the need to turn to the follies of the off-the-peg fashion world. These excellent and artistic designers made everything that was needed for whatever event, tour or engagement, in a thoroughly regal fashion.

The couturier then had to adhere to certain rules. No evening dress in fine or delicate fabrics could be made without a little reinforced patch behind the breast.

This was to take the weight of decorative medals or brooches that were inevitably worn. The design of an evening dress was also rather limited as a number of gowns were worn with sashes draped across the bodice, not an easy effect to be incorporated when deciding on shape, fabric and detail. Evening gowns were required, with so many decorations and jewels, to be rather dignified.

Now, however, the highlight of any grand evening occasion with either the Duchess or the Princess attending will be the dress. With two young Royals to follow, fashion interest is now firmly centred on what creative ideas the latest gown will incorporate.

The Duchess of York has already raised eyebrows by shopping at

the brilliant French couturier Yves St Laurent. But when it was seen that the result of her style and his genius at cut and form was so clearly better than anything she had worn before, she was not only forgiven but Royal fashion watchers eagerly awaited the next romantic and feminine creation the master would create for her.

Another successful design partnership for the Duchess has been with Alistair Blair. She chose his heavy Duchess satin gown in ivory, black and blue for an official portrait by the photographer Terence Donovan before her wedding. This dress was later copied for her likeness at Madame Tussauds, the famous waxworks exhibition in London. Sarah does not always seem happiest in frills and flounces, although the bow, back pleat, bustle and peplum all enjoyed a revival in the fashion world after the Duchess began wearing them. Something she refuses to change, it seems, is her love of more fearsome pursuits; the tomboy, perhaps, will always be there. She looks terrific in a flying jacket and roughwear. However, in contrast, shortly before taking off in a canoe for a two-week holiday under canvas with her husband in the North West Territories of Canada, she attended a dinner in Edmonton in the most romantic silk tulle and chiffon ball gown decorated with ribbons and pearls, looking like every little girl's fantasy of a Royal Duchess. Her dress was a work of art by Zandra Rhodes.

Similarly, the Princess of Wales has some stunning evening clothes designed by Victor Edelstein, Bruce Oldfield and Catherine Walker of the Chelsea Design Company. Catherine Walker, in particular, has come near to the old arrangement of personal couturier to Diana, creating beautiful clothes with simplicity and elegance, while making them totally suitable for each engagement. This was never better executed than when the Princess, together with Prince Charles, went to a gala night in Cannes, in the South of France, to honour Sir Alec Guinness. Nobody there could fail to be impressed by the remarkable combination of regal charm and true Hollywood style that floated into view as Diana arrived in soft blue chiffon. Especially the men who constantly dance attendance—the world's press photographers.

24

3 Royal Designers

Philip Somerville, milliner
A New Zealander who left his home there 26 years ago to visit London, and decided to stay, he worked for the creative and brilliant Otto Lucas in the Sixties as his sales manager and personal assistant. Otto had a succession of high society clients including the immensely stylish Duchess of Windsor, so the Royal connection is hardly new to Philip Somerville. His clients include the Princess of Wales and the Duchess of

York, the Duchess of Kent and Margaret Thatcher. He has both a ready-to-wear collection and a couture collection every year, using only the finest materials to complement the latest fashions. Many fashion designers commission Philip to work on specific designs for their collections.

Graham Smith, milliner.
Graham was born in London in 1938. He studied at Bromley College of Art and the Royal College of Art, after

Philip Somerville holding the hat that the Princess was to wear in Berlin.

which he spent a year working for Lanvin in Paris. When he returned to London, it was to create hats for couturier Michael. He worked for himself for the next fourteen years until becoming Design Director at Kangol in 1981, although he continues to design his own model collection. His individual style is worn by a distinguished clientele, including both the Princess and the Duchess, and two of his designs for the Pirelli Calendar are now held by the Fashion Department of the Victoria and Albert Museum.

Alistair Blair, designer
Born and educated in Scotland, Alistair Blair came to London in 1974 to study at St Martin's School of Art. After attaining a first class honours degree, he took up the position of assistant to Marc Bohan at Christian Dior Couture. He then spent two years at Givenchy

The Princess of Wales honouring the Germans by wearing the Somerville hat and a startling yellow and black checked coat by Escada. She rarely wears anything other than British clothes on official engagements but this was a diplomatic exception.

27

Graham Smith, who makes hats for both the Princess and the Duchess received a rare handwritten 'Thank you' letter for this hat. He had completed it by hand in order that it was ready for the visit to Britain of King Fahd of Saudi Arabia in March 1987. The Royal Hussar, cream and gold braided suit and the Cossack hat made a perfect match.

Roland Klein, successful designer of easy daywear that perfectly suits the mood of every season, always with a theme and a little bit of wit, like his trompe l'oeil sweater with pleated skirt at polo. The Princess loves his designs for official and off-duty occasions.

Alistair Blair, surrounded by his many designs for spring/ summer 1988.

This is the first Alistair Blair outfit the Princess of Wales wore in public, distinctively marked by the AB and the thistle motif on the black and white checked jacket buttons.

The Duchess of York in her favourite double duchess satin fabric. Since she started having dresses like this one designed by Alistair Blair, this fabric has been in such demand the suppliers of the material have had difficulty coping both here and in France.

Diana in Venice in a favourite green coat with square collar designed by the Emanuels for the Italian tour in 1985.

Above:
Fabulous gowns with a fairy tale fantasy woven into them are the work of Elizabeth and David Emanuel. Here they discuss the designs for the Gulf tour with the Princess at Kensington Palace as part of the ITN documentary 'In Private, In Public'.

Left:
Sarah in a beautiful Emanuel gown. It has a boned bodice in black silk satin and a white organza skirt with fabulous black embroidery.

Catherine Walker, currently the leading Royal designer, makes for all the family. The Princess of Wales had the wonderfully inventive idea of commissioning a matching coat to Prince William's from Catherine. It was a copy of a little yellow coat that Prince Charles wore as a child. And now Henry has one too! The fabric, a soft blue wool flannel, was also made up into a man's trilby shape but with wider brim by Philip Somerville, who suggested she borrow the riding stock and pin from Prince Charles!

and in 1980 moved to Chloe to work as assistant to Karl Lagerfeld for three years. Back in London in 1985, he started his own label backed by international entrepreneur Peder Bertelsen. His first collection was given international acclaim and his clothes are now worn by such elegant customers as the Duchess of York; the Princess of Wales, Faye Dunaway and Whitney Houston. He believes that 'simplicity is the art of decoration'.

Roland Klein, designer
Born in Rouen in 1938, he studied at L'Ecole de la Chambre Syndicale alongside Scherrer and Guidicelli. After college he went to work for Dior between 1960 and 1962, then to Patou as Karl Lagerfeld's assistant. He left Paris in 1965 and came to London to join the firm of Marcel Fenez. As managing director, with his own label, he opened his own shop in London's Brook Street in 1979.

Lindka Cierach, designer.
Born in 1952 in Lesotho, South Africa, to a Polish father and an English mother, Lindka moved with her family to Uganda in 1954 and six years later started school in England. In 1972 she left England and, after a brief visit to Italy and nine months in Paris, returned to the family home in Cornwall. Her love of fashion took her to *Vogue* magazine where she worked until it was suggested she should take a course in design at the London College of Fashion. A star pupil, she

had a brief spell as an assistant to Yuki in London and Paris, then started working on her own. In 1985 a prophetic report on her work by *Tatler* magazine named her as the 'hottest society dressmaker'. In 1986 she was commissioned to design the wedding dress for Sarah Ferguson, now Duchess of York. In March 1987 she showed her first ready-to-wear collection at Gieves and Hawkes, the renowned tailors in Savile Row.

David and Elizabeth Emanuel, designers
Elizabeth was born in London in 1953 and David in Bridgend, Wales, in 1952. They met at Harrow School of Art and were married in 1975, becoming the first married couple to study at the Royal College of Art. Their final presentation, made totally in white, became legendary and Browns, the well-known and immensely chic shop in South Molton Street, London, immediately showed interest. This inspired the couple to open their own establishment, showing their first collection in September 1977. Their clientele reads like a showbiz Who's Who—including Elizabeth Taylor, Bianca Jagger, Jerry Hall, Jane Seymour, Shakira Caine, Marie Helvin and many more. But the most spectacular client for the Emanuels has been the Princess of Wales. As Lady Diana Spencer she commissioned them to produce the sensational bridal gown that 700 million TV viewers saw in 1981. They designed the major part of her wardrobe for her visit to the Gulf and appeared with her in an ITV documentary, 'In Private—In Public'. More recently, they have designed outfits for the Duchess of Kent and for the tour of Mauritius undertaken by the Duchess of York.

Arabella Pollen, designer
Arabella started her own design collection for private customers in 1981, forming her own wholesale company later that year. In 1984 Arabella was chosen to design the uniforms for Virgin Atlantic. She shows with the London Designer Collection twice a year and sells her collection to shops throughout Europe, the Far East and the States. The Princess of Wales is her most celebrated customer.

Jasper Conran, designer
Born in London in 1959, Jasper attended Bryanston School until, at only 16 years old, he won a place at Parson's, the world-famous design school in New York, between 1975-1977. He went to work first with Fiorucci and then with Wallis, before putting his own collection and show together in 1978. He was known as the 'enfant terrible' of the British fashion scene until it became apparent that this did not stop him producing high fashion tailoring in a simple and brilliantly wearable way. The Princess of Wales has several examples of his expertise in both her public and her private wardrobes.

Bruce Oldfield, designer
Born in London in 1950, he was taken into the care of Dr Barnardo's nursery home in 1951 and then fostered at 18 months old by a dressmaker and tailor, Miss Violet Masters. In 1963 he went back to Dr Barnardo's to continue his education at Ripon Grammar School in Yorkshire, and later began a three-year teacher's training course in Sheffield. In 1971 he moved to London to take a fashion and textile course at Ravensbourne College and in 1972 transferred to St Martin's School of Art. From 1972 he began to make his mark, winning the prestigious Saga mink competition and gaining commissions to design clothes for the 'Charlie' promotion with Revlon. His first solo show was held in the Plaza, New York, after being invited to the States by the influential store Henri Bendel. In 1975 Bruce started his own company in London and began to sell to all the most sophisticated stores across the world. In 1983, following an increasing demand by private clients for his couture design, he began to concentrate more and more on making unique glamorous evening dresses and elegant day wear for a rich and beautiful international clientele, including the Princess of Wales. He opened his first shop in June 1984.

David Sassoon, designer of Bellville Sassoon, founded in 1953
David joined Belinda Bellville from the Royal College of Art, where his work had been impressive. Belinda had

Lindka Cierach, the designer of the Royal Wedding dress.

Right:
The Puritan collar designed in several early Princess of Wales dresses by Jan Van Velden. They were much loved by the Princess and the public, who bought them for many seasons.

Victor Edelstein, whose grand designs have been an enormous success. The most dramatic was a midnight blue, velvet off-the-shoulder gown worn by the Princess of Wales to a dinner at the White House in 1985, given by President and Mrs Reagan. The Princess subsequently danced with John Travolta.

been involved as a deb in a Bond Street shop, had worked on a magazine and had assisted a fashion photographer before founding her own company. They are now partners and extremely successful, especially with their work for the Royal family. David Sassoon has designed clothes for both the Princess of Wales and the Duchess of York. Other Royal clients include Princess Margaret and the Duchess of Kent. He is proud of his succession of firsts for the Princess of Wales. Originally introduced to her by her mother, who was a client, he made a great many of the Princess's engagement clothes and her going away outfit. He also designed her first Opening of Parliament gown, her first outfit for the Remembrance Day service at the Cenotaph, her first coat for Christmas with the Royal Family and a complete maternity wardrobe for her pregnancy while expecting Prince William.

Jan Van Velden

Jan was born in Amsterdam in 1941. He attended fashion college in Amsterdam and the London College of Fashion. His first Royal commission was for the Princess of Wales, for her tour of Australia in 1983. He has also designed outfits for Princess Michael and the Duchess of Kent.

Victor Edelstein

Born in London in 1954, Victor trained at various fashion companies such as Alexon and Salvador. He was with Biba during the heyday years of the late 1960s and then moved on to work for Jorn Langborn at Christian Dior, London, from 1976 until 1978. On leaving Dior, he set up by himself in Covent Garden, making ready-to-wear clothes. However, his thoughts soon reverted to making couture outfits for private clients, and five years ago he moved his business to Stanhope Place, Kensington.

Victor's first Royal commission was a high-waisted, pink taffeta maternity evening dress, designed for the Princess of Wales while she was expecting Prince William.

The shimmering Bruce Oldfield pleated gold lamé dress the Princess ordered for the Dr Barnardo's Ball which raised £40,000. The gold dress put gold firmly on the fashion scene for that Christmas.

Arabella Pollen designed this single-breasted suit in hunting pink and black. The Princess has worn it many times and with its scalloped hemline it is a clear favourite.

The beautiful hand-painted pale blue chiffon dress by David Sassoon. A favourite of the designer's and obviously of Diana's, she has worn it five or six times since it first appeared at the Gonzagas exhibition at the Victoria and Albert Museum.

Right:
Typical of his expert tailoring, Jasper Conran designed this dramatic white suit for the Princess of Wales for her visit to Tasmania.

4 Working Wardrobe

Special-occasion dressing takes on a much larger dimension when applied to the Royal workload. The working wardrobe needed for daytime has to be memorable, and almost without a fault the Princess and the Duchess have achieved this. However, their working wardrobe is often judged on a very fundamental level, especially by the press.

The Princess and the Duchess are said to make mistakes, but who judges those mistakes and are they really qualified to do so?

Hardly anyone in these media circles has, at the point of comment, actually seen the garment, the fabric or the impact it may have had during that particular Royal visit. All this attention has meant that the working wardrobe for these two young Royals has had to become almost theatrical.

A two-edged sword, this may satisfy the new, almost voracious appetite of fashion gossip that has built up around these two Royals. But it also has created headlines all over the world making our Royal family as well known as the Dallasty families, bringing with it an over-zealous papparazzi and an unseemly desire to strip the Royals of their mystery, their mystique.

Amazingly Diana at only 26 and Sarah at only 20 months older seem to have matured while having to hold this image on the world stage. Simultaneously, they both have had to play an enormously important role whilst taking the responsibility of choosing suitable clothes—outfits that will bridge the gap between that which is appropriate and clothes that are glamorous—without being seen in anything flashy or over-designed.

Western society is very used to judging people, Royal or otherwise, by their clothes. Both their Royal Highnesses have had to learn very quickly the art of dressing for engagements as diverse as pop concerts in aid of various charities, formally

Above:
Miss Evelyn Dagley brings the Princess her outfit to be worn later in the day at the Royal Botanical Gardens, Melbourne. The outfit was one of many in her charge during the official tour of Australia in Autumn 1985.

meeting heads of state, or, in the case of the Princess, inspecting the troops of a regiment of which she is Colonel-in-Chief. On one of these visits she even drove a tank!

It requires very careful thought and planning. Wearing the same garment at two British functions may not be very tactful, but clothes bought specifically for a tour abroad can be very useful for engagements later in the UK.

Outfits originally designed for either Diana or Sarah are carefully 'logged' at the Palace in order that they may be used as much as possible as part of their working wardrobes around the country.

Neither the Princess nor the Duchess is a fashion addict. Anyone with a fervent desire to talk about, plot and plan a special-occasion wardrobe would take at least two hours with, say, their milliners. Royal milliners are lucky if they get 15 minutes with either Diana or Sarah. Both girls know exactly what they want, although suggestions, sketches and fabrics are vital in making up their minds. They are both very aware of the importance of an outfit for a Royal engagement, so careful planning with chosen designers is essential, working out exactly

Right:
This red wool crepe coat with single button fastening, designed by Jan Van Velden, was worn by the Princess on leaving hospital after the birth of Prince Henry.
Slimmed down, the coat was perfect for Melbourne.

Left:
Arriving at the Rock Garden
Restaurant, Covent Garden, in
November 1986, Princess
Diana looks immaculate in this
mandarin collared black and
white suit.
There she presented awards for
Westminster City Council's Anti-
Drug Campaign.

Below:
*Probably the Princess' most
elegant suit. Designed by
Catherine Walker in floral print
silk, the jacket is figure-hugging
with pointed peplum hemline,
puff shoulders and a straight
skirt. The cream hat was
designed by Philip Somerville.
The Princess is visiting the
13th/18th Royal Hussars at
Tidworth to present the Guidon.*

what will be needed to make the right impression.

At this stage, sketches and swatches are very necessary.
Designers go to the Palace to discuss the clothes that will be
required and glean as much information as possible about exactly
what the visit will involve and what the Princess or Duchess will
be required to do.

This all helps to make sure the right garment is created. In
some cases, if there is a suitable outfit for an engagement
already available, all their Highnesses buy is a new hat,
or accessories.

On some occasions the right hat, often originally made for
Ascot, is worn with various outfits within the Royal wardrobe.
Pitfalls are, as far as possible, ironed out at the design

Above:
*Visiting a Japanese car factory
during the offical tour in
May 1986. The suit in peach
silk cloque has a three-quarter
length jacket and straight
skirt and was designed by
Bruce Oldfield.*

The Princess at a fashion school in Belfast during a one-day visit to Northern Ireland in October 1985.
The look, with pie-crust frill blouse and small pert hat, is reminiscent of her early days.

stage—difficult hemlines for getting in and out of cars must be avoided. Clothes may sometimes be required to fit happily under overalls. Extra long or voluminous sleeves could well get in the way of machinery should either one of them wish to get really involved at a new factory. Clothes must not be too tight in case one of them should wish to crouch down to chat to the elderly or sick, or to groups of little children. All this and, of course, the rather unpredictable British weather, must be taken into consideration.

It falls to the Royal dresser, Miss Evelyn Dagley, to make sure that these engagements are planned perfectly beforehand for the Princess of Wales. A loyal member of the Royal household, she is

Above:
The Prince and Princess of Wales arriving at the Expo 86 Exhibition in Vancouver, Canada. Diana wears an elegant fitted coat-dress by Catherine Walker in red and black pinstripe wool with the new basque waistline.
Her 'back of the head' Breton hat in the same fabric is by Graham Smith.

46

Right:
A fine wool flannel black spotted seven-eighths coat with a matching silk satin blouse with flock spot. The Princess of Wales saw the outfit at a British fashion show in Vienna and had her Lady-in-Waiting, Anne Beckwith-Smith, ring to order it for her tour of Canada. The matching satin cobalt blue hat was by Graham Smith.

Above:
Neat the suit might be, but the peplum rides up just like anybody else's! The Princess of Wales making some final adjustments as she enters the 1985 Ideal Home Exhibition.

in her early thirties and was formerly housemaid in Buckingham Palace. However, the Princess takes a great deal of interest personally in the actual liaison with designers throughout the planning.

When she had to change from a well-dressed Sloane Ranger to the first Princess of the land, she had help from fashion experts at *Vogue* and in particular Anna Harvey. They, after all, had all the latest collections well-documented at the start of the season and could very easily pass on invaluable information about the latest and best designers. She has learned a lot and, in particular, has got to know all the major designers personally, so the assistance, although still an invaluable short cut, is not needed as often as before.

David Emanuel who, with his wife Elizabeth, created her first devastating black strapless dress and, of course, the most important frock of all—her wedding dress—says that over the years they have collected photographs of their work worn by the Princess and at one time had three portraits on their showroom staircase—one taken in 1981, one on the Royal wedding day and one from the Venice trip in 1985. He remarked that you would think you were looking at three different women as she had changed so much physically over the years and goes on doing so. But, he says, her personality has never changed; she is still the same girl they met before she married Prince Charles— 'just wonderful'.

Right:
The Princess at the Malcolm Sargent Concert in aid of Cancer Research in 1983. She wears a beautiful calf-length velvet dress with antique lace collar by Gina Fratini.

Above:
One of the successful Bruce Oldfield designs for the official tour of Italy in Spring 1985. For Venice Diana chose this royal-blue silk crepe dress with black asymmetric waistline.

Other designers marvel at the way she knows every piece of her wardrobe thoroughly. During discussions for a tour, one remarked, you will be talking over a colour or a fabric and she will jump up and immediately return with exactly the right item from her wardrobe.

She is constantly surprising, astounding designers with her knowlege and recall, always kind, amusing and enthusiastic.

None of this, they insist, is because she is particularly interested in everything to do with fashion but because she is so very anxious to do the best possible job dressed in the most appropriate way.

It was typical of the Princess of Wales that when she attended a British fashion show in Madrid she wore a suit by Rifat Ozbek,

Below:
A dramatic moire taffeta peplum suit by Rifat Ozbek for a British fashion show at the Ritz, Madrid in Spring 1987.

Above:
The Princess attending an engagement in Canberra during the 1985 tour of Australia. Her silk crepe dress has small jet buttons at the back and is by Victor Edelstein.

49

who is the nearest designer we have to Yves St Laurent in colour, balance and daring, in a style that had more than just a touch of the matador about it. As this was one of the more flamboyant scenes to steal, Ozbek had pulled out all the stops to produce an opulent turquoise-blue moire silk suit embellished with gold braid.

It is often said that the Queen is the most thrifty when it comes to her wardrobe. However, the Princess of Wales is undoubtedly the most inventive and adaptable when it comes to making her wardrobe really work for her. The cost of it is often guessed at. It can only be a guess as the Princess and the Palace do not have any hard-and-fast rules about payment. It is usual for the Princess, as she is buying direct, to pay a wholesale price. This is the cost of the garment plus labour and Value Added Tax, making all her clothes very cost-effective.

This does not affect the more successful designers or couturiers. However, a small designer working without a backer could not hope to sustain that service—if he or she wished to stay in business, that is! So the Palace is billed for the retail price. This is another difficult decision for that designer, for should they overcharge, then like any other customer the Princess might not come back! This is a hazard of the new Royal openness as designers are chosen as they become fashionable.

Another danger, up until now always avoided by the Royal Family, was the risk of exclusivity being broken.

It was always assumed that a garment made for any one of the other Princesses or Duchesses would be the only one. Diana and Sarah have no such qualms. They will happily attend the collection of a favoured designer, select clothes from the runway and have them made in their size and in their colour choice. In some cases, particularly with Sarah and her trips abroad, there hasn't even been time for that—the clothes have literally come straight off the peg. At no time has a designer been asked to remove a garment from the range or the other remaining styles from the shop.

To a certain extent the Duchess of York does not have the same facilities as Diana within the Palace and she is still feeling her way with her own particular style. Although she has not had the experience that Diana has, she is learning fast.

At the time of her engagement she had the advantage of knowing her own style within the life she led then. She even commented on it during the pre-wedding interview on television, saying she saw no reason why she should change.

But, following her sister-in-law's lead while 'trying not to tread on one another's toes', she has developed a new and quite definite style. This becomes very clear when one compares any present-day pictures of her working wardrobe with her engagement photograph.

To form a Royal look that has the sort of spell Diana has cast on the public takes time and dedication. Sarah with her outwardly boisterous, unruly look, seems to have a long way to

Above:
The Duchess of York in a striking navy and white outfit in Australia in 1988. The collar and buttons give a nautical effect.

go. But then she will never have to compete completely, and as her role doesn't carry the same responsibility, stress and strain, it will always be more relaxed. It is already clear that she has taken up that part of her role with gusto. She loves to joke with the photographers, and always treats them with good humour. While covering the Royal engagements regularly, one newspaper photographer remarked that, just like the Queen Mother, Sarah will always turn and wave so that you get your picture.

She has a confidence that comes from being a very physical girl. A fine fast skier, an excellent swimmer, she rides expertly like all the Royals for sheer enjoyment and has done so since she could walk. She is brightly involved when it comes to any work that is close to her heart.

She endeared herself to all the Royals by riding the Grand National winner Aldaniti through Windsor Great Park to raise a thousand pounds for cancer research. She joined in all the Royal

Above:
Attending the concert 'Christmas Carols with the Stars' in aid of the Leukaemia Research Fund at the Royal Albert Hall, 1987. The Duchess wears a Chanel dress with small Christmas tree brooch pinned on the left—a jokey accessory typical of the Duchess' sense of fun.

Left:
The Duchess of York at the Banqueting House, Whitehall in May 1987 where she presented the Royal Aeroclub awards. Her outfit is by Yves St Laurent.

51

Left:
A visit to the Red Arrows at the RAF Central Flying School, Scampton, Lincolnshire in May 1987 to mark the 23rd season of the Red Arrows Display Team.

horseplay when at Alton Towers she led her star-studded team into a boisterous game of 'It's a Knockout', again in aid of charity.

Visiting the Red Arrows, she made her enthusiasm really evident. It was clear from the beginning that she wished to understand all there was to know about flying and, of course, was quick to get her wings in both light aircraft and helicopters. With her exuberance showing, she set off across the tarmac with the magnificent men in the red flying machines. She was dressed to match their clear red, in a stylishly cut outfit and wearing red arrows, darts, in her bow-tied ponytail. Her enjoyment was self-evident.

It was around this time that the trimmer, tailored Sarah emerged, showing off a newer look courtesy of YSL in clothes that are, like her, no-nonsense, good humoured, and with a hint of wit about them. The red jacket with her new trade mark, the bow, sewn all over it was an inspired choice. His dusky pink jacket was another winner, in spite of her titian hair. Sarah had begun to find her rightful silhouette.

But not all the bouquets should go to YSL. After a rush appeal for help, the Emanuels closed their shop one night and let Sarah try on anything she liked. It was the start of yet another Royal success with a British designer, and a very easy and quick way to find out just what suited the Duchess and which silhouettes worked especially well on her. This is vitally important when you realise that the working wardrobes of these two important Royal ladies are seen, and have to work from, every angle on official engagements.

She is also beginning to enjoy the dressing-up aspect of the new Royal role. At a recent auction of designer dresses to raise money for Aids research, celebrities modelled expensive gowns as they went under the hammer. A wonderfully theatrical white organza Scarlett O'Hara dress by the Emanuels was modelled by Bianca Jagger, and a photograph had already appeared on the cover of the *Sunday Express* colour magazine before it went up for

auction. A rather surprised David and Elizabeth were subsequently summoned to the Palace to look at it on its new owner—the Duchess of York!

The classic jacket of last autumn was a winner not just with the public but also with both Diana and Sarah.

Fashioned in black and white tweed, with the '87 touch of elegant black velvet collar, both girls appeared in these stylish tailored suits that were, while not from the same designer, almost identical in shape.

Most Royals are rarely seen in black and white with not a hint of colour, however fashionable it might be. The graphic look simply isn't visible enough. It is most important that the Royals are seen as clearly as possible and bright colours really help.

It is also quite remarkable how the Royal redhead has coped with the continuous stream of vivid colours. Redheads are not known for their ability to wear red, yellow, orange or purple, but this particular Royal flame-haired figurehead has defied all the rules and proved just

Below:
Probably one of the highlights of the year for the Duchess, she wears the Red Arrows colours with a favourite black and white roll-necked satin blouse by Alistair Blair.
She was later to loop-the-loop!

Right:
The Duchess of York in October 1987 at St Bartholomew's Hospital, London for the official opening of the Sick Children's Trust 'Home from Home'.

what a load of rubbish some of these fashion rules can be.

It would be typical of Sarah to lightheartedly have a go—you can almost hear her say, 'Rules are made to be broken'.

Right or wrong, other titian-haired girls must be taking great heart from this parade of pastel and brilliant colours, where none are barred.

It must be remembered that it was Prince Andrew who said that Sarah's hair changes colour all the time. Sometimes it is fiery, other times almost blonde, if strawberry blonde. This is all perfectly possible, depending on her biological mood which, like everyone else's, changes weekly. Her hair was a wonderful barometer (as Prince Andrew predicted) throughout her pregnancy. And when, in the last months, she ceased carrying out public engagements and enjoyed wearing off-duty, easy, comfortable, maternity clothes, she

Above:
The Princess of Wales in Munich during an official tour of West Germany in November 1987. She wears a wool and cashmere double-breasted jacket with velvet collar and button cuffs and a skirt gently flaring from the hip. Her white blouse has a buttoned-back collar and a riding-stock style tie.

could do so without criticism.

Until the pregnancy began and maternity clothes had to be thought of, it must be remembered that her look was admired by some very influential designers. The bow and snood worn with a fitted tunic coat and short straight skirt by Alistair Blair was a particularly foward-thinking look as far as fashion was concerned.

Lindka Cierach's navy-and-white silk print dress was an ideal shape for her, with the accent on her shoulders and her neat waistline. It was admired by more than one designer, who wished it had been one of hers!

What will be interesting to watch in the future will be her relationship with British designers versus the obvious mutual delight of being a customer of the French designing legend Yves St Laurent.

The advice of an editor to help with the 'racking' of her working

Right:
The Duke and Duchess of York in pensive mood in Los Angeles in 1988. The Duchess's scalloped top was enhanced by a wide black velvet bow and a simple black skirt.

Above:
Attending an 'Any Questions' luncheon at the Grosvenor House Hotel in aid of Birthright in May 1987, the Duchess of York sports this delightful tomato-coloured silk jacket. Designed by Yves St Laurent, the jacket was covered in the Duchess' trademark—bows.

Left:
A proud and smiling Duke and Duchess of York after the Christening of their daughter, Princess Beatrice, at the Chapel Royal, St James's Palace, in December 1988.
The Duchess wore a green suit by Yves St Laurent, topped by a picture hat designed by Philip Somerville.

Below:
The Duchess of York in her role as connoisseur arriving at the Mall Galleries in 1988.

wardrobe clothes was essential—not necessarily because of her need for style help, but owing to the size of the job, and the need to delegate as much as possible of her working day. Her duties and baby will also need her attention and the schedules revised to make everything easily possible.

Working wardrobes make very hard work, and the Princess and the Duchess would probably defy anyone to work as hard on so many changes in one day to accommodate every event and eventuality.

5 Off Duty

The Duchess of York is wearing a grey cotton tunic blouse from Fenwicks of Bond Street decorated with small teddy bears.
Her pleated 'wicket' skirt is by Ralph Lauren, as is the black crocodile belt.

Far right:
The Prince and Princess of Wales at polo during the Australian tour of 1985. Diana wears a green and white seersucker shirt dress by Chris Clyne.

The pressure of official appearances seems to fade fast when either Sarah or Diana are seen off-duty with their respective husbands and families.

Unfortunately, it seldom means that the pressure is off from the fashion point of view. If there is a camera there, then the casual, relaxed off-duty outfit will be given the same critical treatment by the same commentators, time and time again.

This is hardly surprising as the fashions that the Princess, particularly, has worn have had as much impact on a trend-hungry mass manufacturing market as the formal wardrobe created for her official engagements.

A measure of her perception at picking out and expertly wearing instant fashion ideas is that so many off-duty clothes have been a huge financial success for the British fashion trade, in some cases making the names of otherwise unknown young innovators. The Duchess of York is not far behind in weaving her own brand of personal magic.

She captured everyone's hearts with the informal way she planned her wedding to Prince Andrew and by the time she had climbed into her flower-sprigged, puff sleeved going-away outfit, the feeling of a family affair was totally confirmed.

Besotted with teddy bears, one was arranged to accompany her, almost overshadowing her new husband in size, as the carriage took them from Buckingham Palace on their honeymoon.

She had managed to give an off-duty look to even the most formal of events—a Royal wedding. Titian hair flying, now unrestrained in the way the Duke prefers it, she bounced her way into everyone's affection.

Sarah clearly finds the fashion joke a great way of getting the message across. An action girl at heart, she climbed down from her

Below:
Relaxed and smiling, the Princess of Wales wears one of her new famous baseball caps, jeans and a T-shirt as she watches a polo match.

Piper Warrior having flown from RAF Benson to collect her private pilot's licence and, clearly thrilled with her achievement, wore the complete Biggles outfit of flying jacket over a polo-necked sweater, matching pants with brown suede boots and a long silk scarf. It was a celebratory outfit, right down to the hair clips shaped like biplanes in her plaits.

Far more at home with her casual wardrobe, having suffered so much at the hands of the Royal Style Wars critics over her formal dressing, she looks her best in Ralph Lauren with his Anglo-American aristocratic way of creating fine country clothes.

Strangely, Diana is a country girl at heart, having been raised that way in Norfolk, but because her background is far grander (she was born at Sandringham) than the Duchess, she finds it easier to dilute her elegant regal look off-duty with a casual jacket or shirt, creating a style that has been dubbed casual chic. Some of her silk dresses are so stylish that with the right hat they could easily fit into her working wardrobe.

Diana has a fairly uneasy relationship with horses. She is hardly ever seen enjoying her off-duty time in their company, except when it comes to supporting her husband at his many polo matches. He

plays, and she presents the prizes, usually looking devastating.
Proud of his achievements in this sport, she will bring the whole
family, rain or shine, in what can only be described as
designer separates.

Unlike her official wardrobe, this is often by foreign designers.
Diana is particularly fond of Mondi and Escada co-ordinates from
Germany, and the successful Italian chain Benetton's range of young
separates for herself and her two young Princes.

Naturally these European firms realise that the Princess is unable to
wear their clothes in the execution of her offical duties, but that only
makes them more thrilled and delighted that she chooses them to
wear in her own time. Mondi keep cuttings proudly in Frankfurt and
were particularly pleased that she wore a Mondi double-breasted suit
in bold check for an impromptu, informal visit to comfort the victims
of the Enniskillen outrage last year in Northern Ireland. The clothes
are all personally chosen at the Mondi shop in Harrods.

Anyone who thought they would see her dressed regularly in the
pastel dungarees and the dimity floral blouses she favoured as Lady
Di was underestimating Diana's love of shopping. For once she was
able to extend her spending horizons beyond Laura Ashley and the

Right:
Holding Prince Henry tightly by
the hand, Diana arrives at
Aberdeen Airport in a pleated
skirt by Jasper Conran and
'polo player' sweater by Mondi.

Below:
Diana and Sarah have been
good friends for several years
and enjoy polo together even in
the rain. Here at Windsor in
May 1987, Diana, carrying
Prince Henry, wears the latest
deckchair striped slim-cropped
pants with padded jacket.
Sarah is in a Ralph Lauren
chambray summer dress and
fur collared flying jacket
by Loewe.

Above left:
Prince William's first photocall
in the garden of Kensington
Palace in December 1983.
Millions tried to buy the
all-in-one snow suit with ABC
on the pocket.

less expensive stores in Knightsbridge and wander through the elegant sophistication of stores like Harvey Nichols, she evidently realised that young, easy, casual could also spell beautiful, glamorous and fun.

Co-ordinating several pieces of her off-duty collection herself, Diana loves her calf-length pleated skirts because they are so comfortable, elegant and unrestricting when dealing with two young sons. These are made up for her by Jasper Conran in fine lightweight wool and wool crepe in various colours, to mix and match with the more graphic-designed sweaters, the Polo Player range she owns in navy, green and claret by Mondi.

The Princess has been photographed in both the sweater and the oversized cardigan.

As a mother, she will know the value of brightly-patterned sweaters

when trying to hold her young sons' attention. However, she has been a lover of fun knitwear since before her marriage. She appeared in a Peruvian favourite at Balmoral, cutting a dash even then in green wellies and corduroys. The Black Sheep sweater kept one particular young knitwear firm in business for many seasons. And when pregnant, she emerged at polo in a giant Koala sweater, a wedding present from Australia, amply disguising her condition.

Polo is, of course, very dear to the heart of the Duchess too, not because of her husband but because of her father's connection with the sport. He is the Prince of Wales' polo manager and Sarah has grown up with the game and thus with the Royal family.

As a close 'larky' friend of Diana, she is usually around to lend a hand with the young Princes. It is self-evident that they enjoy one another's company at these informal gatherings, whether it is at polo

63

or skiing, or even in the more formal surroundings of Ascot.

Skiing provided another contrast when Sarah and Diana, with their husbands, were photographed on the slopes together for the first time in Switzerland. Diana looked just like a fashion plate and the Duchess, with skiing as her first priority, wore a technically superb turquoise ski suit. Fiona Smith-Bingham, an old friend of Sarah's together with her husband Kim, imports some of the best ski wear to be bought in the UK.

When pregnant with Princess Beatrice, the Duchess still felt fit enough to ski and be photographed in a fur-trimmed suit, also from friend Fee—as she is known to her close friends.

The Princess became even closer to her friend, Sarah. Diana is a very modern mother, and was an enormous source of knowledge, not only about birth and bringing up the baby—always great fun to gossip about. Diana was the first to break with Royal baby conventions, employing untraditional nannies, schooling her children outside of Buckingham Palace for the first formative years and taking them on tour with her. Sarah knew that Diana's expertise first-hand has made her a 'natural' with children.

The Princess of Wales probably advised the Duchess on the best way to adapt a pregnancy wardrobe to suit sartorial life after birth. But Sarah was able to indulge her favourite fashions of frills and bows when she was out of the limelight in the last weeks of pregnancy. Maternity clothes look better with a youthful prettiness, a femininity that underlines that blessed state of expecting a baby. The Duchess made use of the stores that have known and helped her in the past.

Fenwicks of Bond Street was a store where both Royal girls did their on-the-spot shopping, for everything including lingerie, tights or even toiletries. Without warning, they would both drop in, with a very unobtrusive detective following the Princess, to the delight of staff and customers alike. However, such has been the public's interest in both Diana and Sarah's fashion habits that the store now more and more sends stock to the Palace. This follows a request to send in a selection in different colours of something either of them has seen.

Harrods have an arrangement which lets the Princess shop uninterrupted before the store opens on Wednesdays.

Harvey Nichols do not find it a problem having the Princess in the store during opening hours, saying that they have the kind of customers who would expect to see her shopping there!

The Duchess will always be known for the way in which she makes her own personality tell in her clothing. Whereas the Princess likes a fashion joke, Sarah's are far more personal, like her pudding hat before the Royal baby's presence was announced and her trapper's outfit in Canada in 1987. It was a declaration of free spirit, something she refuses to change, pregnant or not.

Right:
Princess Diana at polo in Cirencester, also with a cardigan draped over her shoulders. She wears a puff-sleeved white shirt with floral printed cotton skirt and is holding a favourite quilted Provencal print cotton hand-bag.

Below:
Looking entirely the part, the Duchess of York at the Windsor Horse Show in May 1987. Sarah loves anything to do with horses.

6 On Tour

A Royal Tour is, by definition, the most exacting of all the engagements undertaken by the Princess of Wales and the Duchess of York. Depending on their schedules, they may have several changes a day during a tour which can last anything from three days to three weeks.

Planned with precision, they involve many hours of discussion and fittings weeks before the departure date, so that the clothes match the mood, the climate, the type of engagement and the circumstances to be encountered abroad while representing Great Britain.

All their clothes and accessories have to arrive immaculately, so the organisation of the Royal baggage is as carefully planned as the designing of the outfits.

Above:
The Royal Luggage.

Right:
Taking the Royal Wardrobe of the Prince and Princess to Australia for the Tour in 1985.

Right:
The Prince and Princess of Wales seen against the splendour of the Emerald Temple, Bangkok, on their visit in 1988. She is wearing an Alistair Blair silk suit—with a suitably emerald green cummerbund.

There is a selection of differently sized and shaped bags to cope with the many outfits necessary for a tour. A wardrobe-sized trunk takes care of the full-length clothing, with each dress wrapped in tissue paper and delicate sleeves padded with tissues in order to keep their shape. Soft blouses and silks are also wrapped in layers of tissue, while hats go in rigid boxes and shoes and jewellery are kept in suede pouches. Every trunk or case is labelled in pink for the Princess or the Duchess and blue for the Prince of Wales. On long trips, outfits are sometimes needed during the flight, so the labels will specifically say so. One story recounts that the Queen asked for an item just before her baggage was about to leave Scotland, for London.

Below:
Receiving a beautiful bouquet, the Duchess of York in Yellowstone, Canada. She wears a stunning daffodil yellow suit in silk faille with white 'polo mint' print. The outfit by Lindka Cierach has a bow-back peplum jacket and full sleeves, which accentuate the Duchess' tiny waist.

Arriving by open landau, the Duke and Duchess at the Woodbine Racetrack in Canada. Sarah is wearing a floral cap-sleeved silk faconne printed dress with a fitted bodice that wraps and fastens with small buttons down one side. The dress, by Lindka Cierach, is teamed with a David Shilling hat with matching flower.

She was told that it had already been packed away. She asked for something else and was given the same answer. The Queen then asked for a Land Rover to come and pick her up, 'Unless, of course, that's been packed away too!'

The preparation of all this is the responsibility of the dressers and the Lady in Waiting. They have the itinerary and are responsible for passing on everything that is known about the tour ahead, right down to working out just how many pieces of baggage will be required. The Princes have this done for them by their valets and their private secretaries. It is then the job of the baggage master on each tour to work out exactly how and when the baggage should be transported. He also decides what is unpacked, and where. Sometimes baggage is organised to stay unpacked until the next stop.

During 1985 and 1986, the Royal Household became computerized, so that an office can now be set up wherever they stop in order to co-ordinate arrangements and keep in touch with Buckingham Palace. This has undoubtedly smoothed the path of this meticulous operation. From this office, all the speeches are prepared and last-minute changes made speedily. There is also a Fax and copying machine so that newspaper reports of the tour which arrive from London, together with any highly confidential documents which are not sent via the Fax, can be made available to all the tour party.

Nothing is left to chance. Even the thank-you letters are prepared in advance on specially headed notepaper available to the Royal party.

There is no doubt that although these tours are very important in terms of Royal flag-waving (the Royal Standard goes too, by the way), they make a relentless workload for the people around the Royal couple. Some of them spend all day and most of the night preparing

clothes, packing and unpacking and making sure there are no mistakes. Often the baggage is only just being put into place on the aircraft as the Royal couple are getting into theirs. Royal tours are fast-moving affairs! This is when the weeks of planning come into their own.

The Princess is nowadays able to relax her planning a little as, after having been on so many trips, she now has an extensive wardrobe to choose from. However, new special-occasion clothes are always needed and, whilst wearing British fashion is always one of her priorities when on tour, this is one of the times when she can perhaps diplomatically choose something from the country she is to visit, like the Escada starkly yellow and black coat on the tour of West Germany. She has chosen fabric that is representative of a country's national flag as a compliment to her hosts, and has taken on board a theme of an engagement very successfully.

This was most marked at a visit to the training ship *Amerigo Vespucci* at La Spezia at the Eastern end of the Italian Riviera during the grand tour of that country in 1985. To accompany Prince Charles in his naval uniform, she wore a neat little nautical hat by Graham Smith and a tailored coat which perfectly complimented the naval flavour of the visit. She pays homage extremely stylishly to the national costume of countries she is visiting and is always particularly shrewd about two aspects of tour dressing. She invariably keeps to the feminine customs of a country, even though she is a Princess, and is very careful to wear her clothes over and over again.

Tours are a splendid indicator of her efforts to save money. In the hands of someone less scrupulous they could be very extravagant and expensive affairs, but both the Princess and the Duchess constantly make use of outfits which have been worn on special occasions such

Above:
The Princess of Wales wearing a hand-painted linen dress by Paul Costelloe when presenting the prizes to delighted winners of a Lifeguards' Competition at Terrigal Beach in Australia in 1988.

*Touring the Gulf in November
1986, the Princess of Wales
fulfills all the required standards
of dress in the country with this
navy and white silk suit.*

Above, right:
*Also in the Gulf, the Princess
wore this pretty rose print
floral outfit with cotton lace
Puritan collar.*

as Ascot, the Derby, Trooping the Colour, Christmas at Windsor or Balmoral, and even the State Opening of Parliament.

Apart from the remodelling of hats, which is mentioned later in the book, the Princess and the Duchess are constantly seen to wear successful outfits repeatedly. This is because they happen to like them personally, or because they know they have been a success with other members of the Royal family or with the general public. It was for this reason that the Duchess was seen again on tour in her going-away outfit, as was the Princess. David Sassoon made two jackets for the cantaloupe silk outfit the Princess of Wales wore when leaving the Palace after her wedding, and it was the long-sleeved jacket that the Princess wore to Australia for her first major tour after her marriage, to keep the sun off her arms.

Sarah's floral printed going-away suit, with long knife-pleated skirt, was back on show during her first tour as Duchess of York to Canada with the Duke. And another 'teddy' appeared — not the cuddly soft toy kind that had been in her open landau as she travelled from the Palace after her wedding, but a 60lb stuffed buffalo head! It happened on a visit to exotically-named Head-Smashed-in Buffalo Jump.

Diplomatic dressing is one newly-introduced aspect of the Royal tour, not just for the benefit of pleasing the host nation but also to extol the virtues of British style abroad. The Royal family belongs to the nation and their first aim is to show everything that is best about our country and to expand the horizons of understanding between nations.

Left:
*This blue and white tunic
with white pantaloons was
designed for the Princess
by Catherine Walker and
worn on the Gulf Tour.*

It has to be said that, given we have two most delightful Royal style stars, it would be unforgivable if the British fashion industry was not helped and represented by their Royal Highnesses. An eyebrow or two was perhaps raised on the day of the wedding of Diana and Charles when one close member of the Spencer family chose to wear French haute couture, even though she was usually a regular customer of Royal couturier Hardy Amies.

It would, of course, be very easy to snub our talent at home. After all, we now consider ourselves as Europeans in the larger context of grand tours to other continents. But the Princess very early on arranged to take on the excellent role of promoting British fashion design at home and abroad when working as a member of the Royal 'firm', and went about the job of learning and getting to know the collections and their designers from the best possible teachers.

It was a totally inspired idea to involve the editor and staff of *Vogue* in those early days. For the very first time the Palace had the British collections vetted, selections made, and 'racking' became a new fashion word. Racking is the preparation of a rack of clothes considered by a fashion consultant to be the most suitable outfits for the forthcoming engagements of a particular customer. It is effectively a fashion-editing task done personally rather than for a readership. The Royal racks contained clothes representative of every designer who *Vogue* believed to be important that season. This turned out to be very important, and was the start of the trend-setting role of the Palace, and in particular, of Diana and latterly Sarah.

Above:
*Seated cross-legged the Princess
of Wales is enjoying a desert
picnic on a visit to the Gulf.*

The Duchess of York in Mauritius in a white silk moroccaine short jacket over a black 'to the knee' skirt and white bustier by Emanuel. She wears a separate black and white striped bow sash and a hat by Marina Killery.

It has been said that Sarah should put herself in the hands of the most important and talented designer in the world, Yves St Laurent, who seems to understand her personality and shape. But that would be a very sad day for British design as she is already proving to be a much-loved and tremendously useful asset to the Royal Family and their international role. She is also unlikely to wish to be dictated to.

Drawing a very careful line between what is acceptable and what is not, occurs for their Royal Highnesses when they are ordering new clothes. It isn't just that on the Gulf tour the Princess of Wales had to hide her elbows and have three-quarter length hemlines, it is also that in the hectic whirl of it all, the representation of British fashion at its best must not be seen to be extravagant in any way. Clothes are never wasted but are packed away and used again, sometimes by other members of the Princess's family when they need to borrow something special, and are constantly up for consideration for new appearances. Skirts have been altered completely in shape, collars removed or added, and accessories used to turn an old outfit, or one worn in pregnancy, into a new look. Both their Highnesses know how to make use of differently styled shirts and blouses to give an extended life to a dress, suit or coat. The fine line of what is

acceptable is then drawn between wearing outfits that have already been seen in another country, or appearing prudent.

An example of this was the green outfit with matching hat that the Princess wore in Australia. It had had an airing in Spain and in the Gulf and might have been thought secondhand for such an important engagement on the occasion of the Bicentennial celebrations. But some very small modifications were made, particularly to the hat, and it emerged looking new, fresh and relaxed.

Diplomatic occasions also pander to the Princess's love of dressing up. In Spain, when she attended the Ambassador's dinner, Philip Somerville made her a mantilla, a fan of plaited tulle and black roses which enchanted the Spaniards. France posed some important decisions, however. They are renowned for their critical attitude towards anything to do with dress, probably because they believe they lead the world in design. The Princess wanted to impress, so she had Philip plan something really special. The brief was to make something new that would not jar with the outfit she intended to

Left:
The Princess of Wales in Madrid in 1987 wearing a Catherine Walker dress and Philip Somerville hat with an unusual and very elegant white bow.

75

Almost unrecognisable, the Duchess of York, with the Duke behind her, as they visit the Yellowknife Mines in Canada.

Left:
The Princess of Wales wore a black and white coat dress with velvet sleeves designed by Catherine Walker at the Matignon Hotel in Paris in 1988.

Below:
The Princess chose a Victor Edelstein pastel pink dress to visit a Surf Festival at Gosford Wharf in Australia in 1988.

wear by Rifat Ozbek; it had to be not too funny, but serious and good looking. Philip made many hats, but it was one with a snood attached which the Princess eventually wore. Her worries were not what the head of Christian Dior might think, but what her hairdresser would say. It was one of the few occasions when she had her hair pulled under her hat. In fact she used hair gel to keep it close to the head, so as not to spoil the line. When the engagement was finished she quickly washed it out before a 'horrified' hairdresser saw it!

Three weeks of planning can often not be long enough when it comes to facing the expert eye and getting every aspect of the outfit to match. One or two of the tour hats have been designed to pick out a spot, a fleck or flower in a certain colour, but when the outfit and hat are photographed together they can 'scream' at one another, to the horror of the milliner.

Left:
The Duchess of York attends a banquet in Mauritius. She wears a black gown with cream duchess satin roses decorating the off-the-shoulder neckline. Designed by the Emanuels, it was dubbed her 'Guinness dress'!

Left:
With Nancy Reagan at the White House in November 1985, the Princess is wearing a midnight blue velvet evening gown by Victor Edelstein.

The Duchess has a very good eye for colour, and wears some particular colours with great aplomb. Bright red and daffodil yellow have been recent favourites on tour, not necessarily assured shades for all redheads but definitely suiting the Duchess of York. With her expert colour sense, she has also been able to wear some accessories with different outfits. For example, a green hat she had originally ordered to match an Ascot dress was a great success when worn with other printed silks in Mauritius. The Duchess is also a great fan of hair decorations and, in a subtly diplomatic way, slipped both the national flower of Mauritius and the maple leaf of Canada under her hat and in her hair to charm both host countries when she visited them during 1987 with the Duke of York.

The very latest lines, the most up-to-date fashion in its grandest state, are perfect for foreign tours.

Because of the splendour of some of the palaces or places of culture visited, a very opulent wardrobe is needed. It is at this point that the very best in British evening clothes comes into its own.

As a nation, that historically has liked to dress up formally, and has had a Royal Family that is seen to do this stunningly on a great many occasions throughout the year, our designers are known for their ability to make some of the most sculptured satins, sheerest chiffons and grand taffetas in the best possible taste! No one is a better advertisement, if we wished for one, than the Princess of Wales.

Her gowns are the perfect balance of fantasy and fashion—and the best example of this is the dress she wore to Washington for dinner at the White House during a Royal visit to America.

It was luxurious yet elegant, and had a wonderful mood of old Hollywood about it. One could almost imagine it as part of the

Above:
As part of a crowded New York programme, the Princess attended a Dawsons International Knitwear Reception in 1989 wearing blue.

Left:
This graphic design in black and white by Catherine Walker was chosen by the Princess of Wales for a Tour of Japan in May 1986.

wardrobe of Elizabeth Taylor in her heyday.

It was also about the time that the trend for framing the shoulders and baring that particular erogenous zone had become fashionable again. So when David Emanuel created the black off-the-shoulder white rosette dress for the Duchess of York many months later, the look, because of its success on Diana, was still setting the pace. The additional white roses he made for the Duchess to wear in her hair were also to herald a new trend for satin roses in the hair, after the black velvet bows had waned a little.

Royal tours are very carefully arranged around the climatic calendar of the foreign countries to be visited. Unless it is vital to coincide with an important date or anniversary the country is to celebrate (like the Bicentennial in Australia) members of the Royal Family are anxious not to travel at the height of summer.

Tours are naturally made up of long days in order for as many different areas and places of interest to be seen and for as many people as possible to meet the Royal Family. It was, of course, very necessary that the Prince and Princess of Wales should be in Australia on the anniversary of the sailing into Botany Bay of the first tall ships re-enacting the landing of the first settlers. It was Australia's hottest

Left:
Meeting the people in Canada. The Duchess wears her maple leaf red and white hat by Graham Smith.

Above:
In a turquoise jacket with her favourite gold buttons, topped by a black hat, the Duchess of York attended Sunday worship at St Luke's Church in Long Beach, USA.

Right:
At the World Expo 1988 in Australia, the Duchess of York gently cradles a koala bear. She is wearing a spotted dress and wide brimmed hat with spotted trimming—and white gloves. Probably she was thinking of Princess Beatrice left behind in England, and the bear looks suitably impressed!

Below:
John Boyd was the designer of this small blue hat which matches a multi-coloured dress worn by the Princess of Wales to attend Morning Service in Sydney in 1988.

time of year.

The Prince and Princess had a tough schedule, and the Princess particularly seemed to be affected by the heat. However it is not for that reason alone that the tours are planned in calmer, less sultry months. Crowds often have to wait for long periods of time in the street, without any shade of shelter, when they wish to see the Royal Family. This was highlighted again on the Australian tour, when Prince Charles said in a speech to the crowd who had waited for him that he thought they had shown great fortitude. Many had collapsed under the strain of sitting in temperatures of over one hundred degrees.

The lighthearted and often humorous side of some of the duties of the Royal Family on their tour around the world makes wonderful reading.

Right:
The Prince and Princess of Wales dancing at the Melbourne High Society Ball in Australia in 1988. Her strapless ball gown was designed by Catherine Walker with a large bow from the hip, and the pinned up hairstyle is a perfect foil for her diamond and sapphire jewellery.

Far left, bottom:
The Duchess of York in black and pink, her hair strikingly netted in a pink spotted matching snood.

However, there is one outfit that is invariably included in the travelling Royal wardrobe. It is essential that a black outfit is always carried as part of the tour collection. This is in case a death occurs or there is a funeral to attend.

During her trip to India, Princess Anne had to attend the funeral of Prime Minister Indira Gandhi after her sudden and tragic death.

The Queen also returned to this country in black from a visit to South Africa in 1952. She had heard at Treetops that her father, King George VI, had sadly died. She was dressed in mourning clothes as she stepped from the plane as the new Queen of England.

Left:
Princess Diana alighting from a river taxi in Venice during the Tour of Italy in spring 1985. She is in the cobalt blue and white suit by Jan Van Velden.

Right:
Barefoot in Mauritius, the Duchess of York climbs from a boat wearing her pink and cream floral print dress by Lindka Cierach.

Most of the travelling around a foreign country is done conventionally by plane or by car. But often the Royals have to take to the water. The Italian tour meant a trip to Venice for Princess Diana, with water taxis and gondolas to negotiate elegantly. The Duchess, in the more informal setting of Mauritius, stepped barefoot from her water transport looking lighthearted and happy, just as Royal tourists should.

7 Hats

It was said of the late and immensely stylish Princess Marina that her large cartwheel-brimmed hats were very unpopular with the crowds, as they obscured her face.

This is probably why 'working hats', as they are known to most members of today's Royal family, have conformed to a small, turned-back, rather unstylish look that really has very little to do with fashion.

As quite definitely the most stylish Princess since Marina, Diana was very careful not to cause the same offence to the public when she first met and then married the Prince of Wales.

She, together with milliner John Boyd, started a trend of shapes much smaller than were usually worn, made in silk and trimmed with bows, feathers or roses.

Another variation of the turn-back brim is worn here by the Duchess as she and her husband visit Scotland in July 1987 as the Earl and Countess of Inverness. Turned back on the side, the crown is decorated inside and out with white silk roses.

The little tricorn hat she wore when leaving Buckingham Palace after her wedding to Prince Charles, the veils, and even the jaunty angle she wore her hats at, were copied throughout the land. They were admired and bought by what seemed to be every bride, bride's mother, aunt, cousin and grandmother. The trade had never had such a fillip. It was a shape that was easy to make, easy to emulate and acceptable to so many age groups.

If it had been thought that her daring black strapless evening gown was a trend setter, that hat shape established her as much, much more. It was evident from that moment that she was to be a major force in representing British fashion abroad. This is a role she has never shied away from, despite the responsibility in one so young and relatively inexperienced in the ways of the fashion world, and the obvious temptations of European design.

A wonderfully glamorous ambassadress, she has simply become more and more knowledgeable, dressing expertly and beautifully in British designer clothing. Any mistakes are quickly forgotten.

The Duchess had to do nothing more than follow her lead and, as far as hats are concerned, has done just that.

Hatters' designs, mad or otherwise, have never enjoyed such a successful period, now that there is yet another young Royal head to

Right:
During her visit to the construction site of the new Parliament House in Canberra in 1985, the Princess later swapped her 'Mary Poppins' style hat for a safety helmet.

Far right:
The Duchess chose a similar style with wide brim and a large bow to wear with a Lindka Cierach dress in Mauritius. The hat by Graham Smith had been designed originally to be worn with a green dress at Ascot Races during the summer.

Below:
A catching eyeveil on a black hat by Viv Knowlands and black coat by Jasper Conran were worn by the Princess of Wales when attending the Armistice Day Service in Paris in November 1988.

dress and a hungry fashion trade to satisfy.

Prior to all the interest in the variety of Royal millinery worn by the Princess and the Duchess, hats were considered a rather dull, if not ageing, accessory—a must for a wedding or a grand occasion, but very little to do with mainstream style in the Eighties.

The Princess and the Duchess have changed all that, and the mass millinery market has been quick to copy every shape in order to meet an overwhelming demand. Nothing, of course, has quite beaten the first little shape, but the Russian toque has come very close.

In the autumn of 1986, the Princess saw on television a hat she admired. Her hairdresser, Richard Dalton, was asked to trace its designer and, through another client of his, Anne Diamond who

For her arrival in Canada in July 1987, the Duchess teamed her elegant red wool suit with this stunning hat by Graham Smith.

presents a breakfast television show for TVAM, discovered that it was made by milliner Philip Somerville. One of the girls from *Vogue* went to see the hat and then the Princess called in to see it for herself. The television version had a veil, and the Princess wanted one with a veil as well. In the first photographs of her wearing it; at a Christmas service back in 1986, the veil was so fine it could hardly be seen. The Princess is very careful with veils, conscious always of the end result in photographs. If it is too heavy, her face cannot be seen properly; if the veil is spotted, it can throw unsightly shadows on her face. It has to be the right weight to appear flattering in a picture, which is why there are now very few veils made for her and why her earlier hats are still being worn but without their original veils.

That cossack hat heralded the start of a long association with Philip Somerville, who then made all the hats worn by the Princess during Ascot week the following summer.

Hats from all the Royal milliners come after the garments are chosen, often in collaboration with the dress designer. Many designers now have their own favourite milliners, so that the Princess and the Duchess are regularly helped with the right style to match an outfit in the form of sketches, or fabrics draped around a block. During these very short consultations, either at the milliner's workroom or at the Palace, the milliner often works with just sketches.

One of the most successful Russian-influenced styles for the Princess was a cream hat that she wore with a complete gold-braided cossack outfit to greet King Fahd in London, on 24th March

Above:
One of Marina Killery's more subdued creations was chosen to top this summery silk dress worn in Mauritius in September/October 1987.

Left:
An unusual hat band on a flying saucer shape by Marina Killery.

The Princess wearing a favourite lavender wool crepe dress and jacket with a Puritan silk crepe de chine embroidered collar by Jan van Velden. The hat is by John Boyd.

1987. The hat had to be made at the very last minute by another Royal milliner, Graham Smith at the House of Kangol. Because of the lack of time, Graham stitched by hand himself and a very appreciative Princess sent him a handwritten letter of gratitude. It is these little touches of perfection that the Princess does so well and so elegantly.

The Duchess is far bolder and has many madcap ideas when it comes to millinery. Her circle of milliners, young and very innovative, has given yet another boost to the design of hats in the Eighties, through their work for the Duchess.

Marina Killery loves a bizarre idea. She is one of many hatters who have worked for the Princess and are now busy with ideas for Sarah. Her enthusiasm for the Duchess is very evident. She is quick to remind all who will listen that Sarah has very little time to devote to

Above:
In January 1988 the Princess of Wales looked stunning in a Catherine Walker dress with navy and white striped silk tie shawl. Her navy and white picture hat is by Philip Somerville.

Left:
Warmly wrapped against the cold, the Princess smiles at her welcome in Glasgow. Her blue outfit and matching hat is enhanced by a white shirt and spotted tie. Could it be one of her husband's?

the rather fanciful world of fashion. Her audiences with Sarah for the Mauritius tour, for instance, had to be very short, sweet and to the point. Sarah was not only working on her book about art, but also preparing for her pilot's licence, which involved a great deal of paper work. Even the Duke was astounded by her ability, but then both projects were of immense importance to her. Hats and clothes in general rather pale into insignificance beside them. However, when she does get inspired she usually has something rather bizarre made. For instance, Sarah always has a fun shooting hat and her Christmas Pudding hat was made for a laugh during the shooting season. The hat like so many of her fun ones, is surreal. Made entirely of felt, it has a white plate with blue edging as a brim, a brown pudding as a crown and a sprig of felt holly as a decoration. Another hoot of a hat that she still has the press guessing about is a white fake-fur 'beret'—which is in fact a perfect curled-up cat. But because she has never been photographed from behind, its little tucked-in face and perfect pink ears have never been documented by the popular press. This trompe l'oeil effect works so well simply because the angle of a jaunty beret, and the one-sided shape a cat makes when curled up, are perfectly matched in this hat. It is outrageous fun—and only Sarah could attend Royal Christmas service at Windsor wearing a cat on her head. Marina loves this aspect of her work and had some of her hats included in an exhibition entitled 'Surrealism in Fashion' at the Institute of Fashion Technology in New York, hopefully transferring to the Victoria and Albert Museum in June 1988.

When it comes to making serious hats for special occasions, Marina again always adds something a little different. Her beautiful dark navy-blue straw hat perfectly complemented a Lindka Cierach dress which the Duchess wore to the races in Mauritius. Marina dressed the hat with real roses and rhododendron leaves, but then felt that the roses were a little too strong in colour. She substituted silk roses in palest pink but kept the leaves, perfectly preserved to be the deepest and most beautiful green. Even then, she decided not to ruin the effect with a hat-band and so she gently twisted the stems around the base of the hat's crown. These hats are more than just 'functional', they are works of art.

The Duchess loves the innovative touch. Someone with less nerve would be rather timid about allowing Marina's unique, rather eccentric, style loose on what is, after all, a world stage.

This was positively demonstrated when the Duchess wore a very unusual Nero wreath made of gold panne velvet leaves for an evening engagement in Canada. The Roman influence came from the pink chiffon dress by the Emanuels which Sarah wore that evening. Marina designed the hat to decorate the one side of the head from temple to the nape of the neck, and the golden ribbons were wired to 'float off'. It is not exactly mainstream millinery, but that bores Marina and, with her love of potty hats, probably bores the Duchess, too.

She has also had hats from David Shilling, another British milliner with a reputation for the unusual. She likes Kirsten Woodward, a young bright-ideas designer who the Princess has also patronised,

94

Above:
This very unusual style of hat was chosen for a visit to Sheffield. The heart-shaped earrings by Kiki McDonough at Nigel Milne were an apt choice.

Right:
The design team of Bellville Sassoon has proved as successful for the Duchess as they have for the Princess and this spotted silk dress worn in Canada is complemented by a stunning picture hat by Siggi.

and British milliners are now enjoying a marvellous exposure by gracing Royal heads of state—literally.

However, there are areas which have to be watched. The Princess, while happy to be seen in big brims, and having height to carry them off well, rarely orders them. She is very aware of meeting dignitaries and overshadowing them, which is typical of her understanding and easy nature. They are also awkward for getting out of cars, while the wind can do wicked things to a large brim. Feathers are also a problem if they are too long. An original beret that Philip Somerville made for a Scottish engagement had to have a few inches taken off by the Princess. She loves trying different styles, although often he will make what she wants and then make what he feels she should have. Sometimes he wins, but mostly Diana knows exactly what she wants.

Fittings also help the milliner to explain exactly how the hat should be worn to maximise the effect. Several hatters have tried to take the Royal hair off the Royal brow, but nobody is going to stop the Princess wearing her hair on her face. She has been persuaded on one or two occasions, but as she dislikes it, her loyal hairdresser, Richard Dalton, is often by her side to help with hat fittings.

Royal hats are often re-pressed and cleaned, trimmings are taken off, and crowns modified to give a longer life to a style so that the Princess can wear it more than once. All this is in line with her aim of giving her very expensive wardrobe a longer life.

A hat is one of the few old-fashioned aspects of the Royal wardrobe still remaining. It is still considered essential for the official working life of any of the female Royal Family, however young.

Hats are important not just in order to make a simple, yet elegant, silk dress look special, but also because they are yet another way of

Another Siggi design tops a yellow and blue suit by Bellville Sassoon worn in Canada.

Right:
The flying saucer hat by Freddie Fox chosen for a visit to Washington in December 1985 is worn with a suit by Catherine Walker that the Princess has worn time after time.

Below:
The Duchess of York in a wonderfully exotic feathered creation worn for Easter Service at Windsor in 1987.

The Duchess of York in rich red Venetian wool jacket and long knife pleated skirt and matching hat. The whole outfit was designed by Edina Ronay as part of the Autumn/Winter collection in 1987. The hat was also by Edina.

This was a hat made by Marina Killery for the Princess of Wales in 1984. It has a black velvet crown and a brim of black seal coney, clipped rabbit and a "V" split back. Marina was congratuated by the Palace.

making our Royal Family more visible in a crowd.

When Philip Somerville was planning the hats for the last Australian tour that the Prince and Princess of Wales attended for the Bicentennial celebrations, he remarked that one hat could easily be worn off-duty. The Princess was almost horrified. She never wears a hat off-duty if she can help it.

There will be very few women who could blame her!

8 Royal Jewellery

The young stars of the Royal family shine even more brightly when the occasion warrants the real family jewels, with tiaras.
Sparkling from their pride of place on perfectly dressed hair, tiaras are quite the most superlative accessory to any of the Royal evening gowns.

They also serve as a reminder that, however young and funny Diana and Sarah can be, they are, after all, their Royal Highnesses. They are both, like their tiaras, part of our heritage.

When the Princess of Wales appeared at her first State Opening of Parliament in the November after her marriage to Prince Charles, she was wearing in public for the first time the spectacular tiara given to her by the Queen as a wedding present.

The tiara is stunning enough, but its history matches anything it can effect in beauty.

It was originally called the Cambridge Lovers' Knot Tiara. The lovely adornment we see today is a copy, made for Queen Mary by Garrard, the Crown jewellers, in 1914. The original was owned by her grandmother, Princess Augusta of Hesse, who married the first Duke of Cambridge, hence the romantic name.

Queen Mary left the tiara to the Queen in its altered state - the original tiara had many upright pearls above the diamond lovers' knots as well as below them—and Princess Diana now takes great pride and care in giving it dignity whenever it is worn.

In 1985, while on an official visit to Washington, she wore the tiara with a stunning lace dress by Murray Arbeid together with pearl and diamond drop earrings which were another wedding gift, this time made by the Royal jewellers, Collingwood.

Collingwood are also the Spencer family jewellers and the Spencer tiara which Diana wore on her wedding day still remains family property. It dates back to the nineteenth century and is a pretty

Top:
In full 'dress' for a banquet in Hobart, Tasmania, the Spencer tiara is teamed with a diamond necklace in the shape of the Prince of Wales feathers, given as a wedding present and the Family Order brooch.

Above:
This gift by the Sultan of Oman was envied by many when the Princess wore the necklace, earrings and matching bracelet.

design of leaves and flowers. Both her sisters have worn the tiara on their wedding days, although nowadays it is the Princess who regularly needs to borrow it.

The Royal Family Order, which the Princess wears on many of her official engagements, is worn with evening dress or on State occasions. Worn on the left side, it is attached to a square of fringed moire silk. The new Family Order is established at the start of each monarch's reign and is given only to female members of the immediate family. The names of those receiving it are never published, and the public only know of the honour once the recipient is seen in public wearing the delicate portrait painted on ivory and surrounded by diamonds. The Princess received it in November 1982, nearly a year and a half after her marriage.

Her clever trick with a necklace on her visit to Australia in 1985 was a shocker to everyone. It must have pleased her hugely, for the paradoxical fact about the Princess of Wales is that, while she seems to be shy on the one hand, she loves to cause a stir on the other! Her dance with Charles in the one-shouldered dress was documented everywhere, this time not because of the dress but because of what she had done with her necklace.

The necklace itself has a wonderful history. Queen Mary had a necklace of the Cambridge emeralds redesigned in the fashionable Art Deco Style of the period in 1927. The diamond-encircled stones were each divided by diamond plaques, with an emerald in the centre. This choker was bequeathed to the Queen, but she never appeared wearing it and in 1981 gave it to the Princess of Wales as a wedding gift. Something inspired Diana to have it mounted on a velcro band and wear it to a Christmas party, which must have been a success as she then showed it to everyone at an Australian charity function while on tour with Prince Charles.

Top, right:
A stunning mass of soft titian curls is the perfect hairstyle by Denise McAdam for this formal occasion requiring a tiara. The hair at the sides is swept up to conceal the band of the tiara.
Above:
Murray Arbeid designed the cream lace evening dress worn on this formal occasion with the Family Order brooch. The tiara was a wedding present from the Queen.

Right:
Although many people thought this pearl and gold pendant necklace was a wedding gift when the Duchess wore it for her big day in July 1986 it had in fact made its appearance before then.

Below:
This choker necklace worn with black ribboned earrings in Mauritius was designed by Kiki McDonough at Nigel Milne.

Above, left:
The Princess and the Duchess have worn similar twisted pearl necklaces and here the Duchess has teamed hers with pearl drop earrings for Ascot 1987. The polo mint suit by Lindka Cierach is topped with an elegant picture hat by Freddie Fox.

The Duchess of York, on the day of her wedding, concealed her tiara behind a wreath of roses, gardenias, lily petals and lilies of the valley. However, when she emerged from signing the register the flowers were gone and we saw her diamond tiara borrowed from a close friend of the Ferguson family. Her entrance at an official engagement in Canada in July 1987 was nothing less than glittering as she showed off the diamond suite of earrings, necklace and bracelet in a beautiful cluster design, the Queen's gift to Sarah on her wedding day.

Below:
The Princess's version of the twisted pearl necklace is worn during a visit to Norway, with pearl drop and diamond earrings and an elegant red-ribboned lace and sequinned evening dress by Jan Van Velden.

Left:
Although admired by many as a daring and apt gimmick, this pearl rope worn knotted down the back for the premiere of 'Back to the Future' in December 1985 caused the Princess a lot of discomfort while sitting through the film.

Above, right:
Her sapphire and pearl choker was an excellent choice by the Princess when teamed with this midnight blue evening dress by Victor Edelstein for a banquet in Vienna in April 1986. The Princess looked a picture of elegance.

Certain likes and dislikes immediately become apparent when looking at the jewellery of the Princess of Wales and the Duchess of York.

The Princess will not wear brooches ... yet. 'People keep trying to make me to, but I won't' she is alleged to have said defiantly. She feels they are 'old' and there is, after all, plenty of time for her to learn to love them. Saving fashions until you feel you are the appropriate age is a clever and stylish trick! She makes an exception when a brooch has a special significance, such as the brooch given to her by the Royal Hampshire Regiment, of which she is Colonel-in-Chief.

The jewel she clearly does favour is the pearl. From the moment she left Buckingham Palace on her wedding day, wearing a five-strand pearl choker with a large pearl and diamond clasp and a pearl drop pendant which she had borrowed from her eldest sister, Lady Sarah McCorquodale, she has put pearls back on the fashion scene. Copies of that particular choker immediately packed display cabinets in the department stores. But that wasn't to be all. Princess Diana cleverly converted her wedding gift from Queen Elizabeth the Queen Mother—a gigantic oval sapphire surrounded by diamonds—into the centrepiece of a seven-row pearl necklace. Her 'Back to the Future' fashion joke, with a long pearl rope knotted down her back, was however a fake. It came, together with a little pearl choker with turquoise stone clasp, and pearl hearts on a little silver bow, from costume jewellers Butler and Wilson.

The Duchess does not have the same problem with brooches. In fact she wore a quite spectacular bow brooch, borrowed from the Queen, at her first appearance at the annual Braemar games in the Scottish Highlands just two months after her wedding to the Duke of York. She pinned it to her blouse and proudly wore her tartan, that of Countess of Inverness. Garrard made this feminine piece in 1858 out of several hundred diamonds supplied by Queen Victoria. In fact there were three bow brooches—two large and one small.

The Duchess loves pearls and has a twisted pearl necklace and drop pearl earrings which were one of her wedding presents. Her favourite piece of all is a diamond and pearl pendant that she wore at her wedding. Wearing it as she does so proudly at every occasion possible, it is clearly a reminder of that wonderful day.

Gifts were showered on Sarah on the birth of her first child in August, as the Royal family loves to pass on heirlooms at the time of weddings or births.

Presents from friends who know her, and relatively inexpensive little gifts she buys herself from Butler and Wilson, Theo Fennell or Eric Beaumon, tend to be semi-precious animals. Her love of teddy bears, panthers, and bees is well known. Add to that the snake Princess Diana wore on her jodhpur tuxedo by Jasper Conran, and her love of little butterflies, and you have a positive zoo of Royal gems!

It is, however, the hairdos of the Royal duo that have become just as rivetting to the public.

Comparing them, Princess Diana's hair is neat and suitable, while the Duchess of York's is a constant source of wonderful colours and splendid ideas both within it and on it.

An identical visit to Canada's historic Fort Edmonton in Alberta was one of the few shared experiences of the Princess and the Duchess, and also one of the few times that any comparisons can be made about the relative merits of their personal taste. As a natural redhead, Sarah favoured a flamboyant neckline, a bright colour and opulent jewellery. Diana chose a high necked, young girl's gown with a modest hat and an altogether more subdued, demure silhouette.

Stepping back into the past and dressing up in the style of the late

Top, left:
Heart shaped earrings and bows are very popular with the Duchess. This pair, designed by Sarah Booth, are gilt bows with crystal and diamante encrusted heart-shaped drops. A panther brooch was chosen for the Chanel suit

Centre, left:
Inverness tartan was no surprise choice when the Countess of Inverness paid a visit there in July 1987. The favourite teddy bear brooch was her own addition.

Below:
Not perhaps a likely choice for the Duchess but a snake by Butler and Wilson is chosen

with a 'jodhpur' dinner suit by Jasper Conran worn for a pop concert in Vancouver in May 1986 by the Princess

Bottom, left:
Butterflies are the Princess's choice for earrings and necklace for this engagement on her visit to Canada. The hat is by Graham Smith.

Right:
For the total look, a black and white pearl necklace with a bee motif was chosen to match this black and white suit by the Emanuels and a matching wide-brimmed straw hat. Bees also featured in the train of the Duchess's wedding dress.

1800s is a fun idea open to all VIP guests at this historic site. Both Sarah and Diana visited the fort, a reconstruction of those early days, as part of their official tours of Canada. The invitation to visit and barbecue clearly states that one must dress in Klondike fashion, which includes bustles, tight bodices, ostrich feathers, dolly bags and lace-up boots. All this was on hand for the Duchess to choose from a VIP wardrobe. However, the Princess of Wales decided to come prepared and had borrowed her pink lace outfit from the BBC's television wardrobe.

It clearly illustrated the difference in style, both in choice of colour and design, between the two girls.

The Duchess's hair was just right for the period. It tumbles about, the envy of anyone who sees it, and has proved inspirational to her hairdresser, Denise McAdam, who until the beginning of the year was working for Royal hairdresser Michael Rasser in his salon, Michaeljohn of Albemarle Street.

Left:
The Princess of Wales arriving at Claridges with the Queen and other members of the Royal Family for the State Banquet given by the President of Nigeria during his State Visit to England in May 1988. Her dress was created by Catherine Walker for the Gulf Tour.

Right:
A smiling and happy Duke and Duchess of York in Paris in the summer of 1987.

Denise, who is married to a builder, Chris Arnold, lives in Surrey. She travels with the Duchess whenever she is needed and copes with the endless stream of ideas the Duchess has about her own hair styles. It is as if she has had all these fantastic ideas caught up in a time warp while she lived the relatively unsophisticated life before Andrew, and now that she is a Duchess she can let rip.

Denise admits that these endless fun ideas with Sarah's titian locks 'just happen'. They admit that 'they trust one another', which is apparent to all as they seem always to work, however startling the change.

Having a sympathetic hairdresser who can interpret everything that you have locked away in your imagination must be a wonderful bonus, particularly when, as a Royal visitor, you are expected to

change several times a day to suit the venue and the hour. Together they have seldom put a curl wrong.

It has to be said that Sarah has a head of wonderfully natural curls. And when they are left to go their own wonderfully wild way, some would think her hair is at its best. This leaves apart the colour which has always been considered seductive.

Attending polo at Windsor with her family and in-laws signals a day of relaxation for the Duchess. Happy among the horses, she always looks like a thoroughly down-to-earth country girl. When duty calls, as it has so many times throughout the last two years, she and her hairdresser are ready for anything. They have used ribbons, bows, kinks and feathers. They have braided and straightened, made ringlets, victory rolls, French pleats and knotted the royal redhead.

She has had little bows, big bows, Christmas bows and baby biplanes in her plaits. She has dressed in an upswept style with exquisite gems and made a tiara look as though it had been put their at birth.

Diana, on the other hand, is growing her hair, as was seen to splendid advantage on the recent Australian tour with the Forties pleat, and all the splendid jiving!

Over the many years since that simple bob at the time of her wedding, she has had her swept-back layered hairdo changed very little. Her hairdresser Richard Dalton, who has become a firm but unlikely confidant over the years, is very conscious of care and condition since the Princess, as a keen swimmer, blow-dries her hair so regularly.

Several years ago he gave up his job at Headlines, in London's Sloane belt, to concentrate on the demands of dressing Diana's hair, and has had spectacular success.

His success is that, given this controlled hairstyle, there are so many different looks on so many diverse Royal dates and all are perfectly in keeping with both the occasion and Diana's own personal style.

His predecessor and boss, Kevin Shanley, had a wife and family, and since the Princess often needed her hairdresser on duty with her from early morning till late at night it was not easy for him. Richard was one of Shanley's stylists and from time to time had helped out with urgent calls from the Palace. It seemed a natural appointment and has been a very good partnership.

Princess Diana's hair has been copied as often as her clothes, and this is probably because it is so simple and elegant, so easy for any head of hair. It would be nigh on impossible to emulate Sarah's as it is so rare to have that colour and that thickness of tresses.

However, Diana's hair has never let her down. Some may not have exactly loved her 'rocker' style when she cut it really short, and when she grew her hair longer after the birth of Prince Henry—drawing it back with combs—the newspapers had a field day, running 'for' and 'against' features.

It is obviously impractical now for her to change into someone with tumbling unruly blonde curls. It is not altogether certain it would suit her and, apart from being useful to put up under tiaras, would not be the Princess so many have come to know and love.

Above:
A dazzling entrance by the Duchess at the Royal Opera House, June 1987, her hair rolled and pinned with pearls.

Right:
Another wonderful hairdo—ringlets dressed with a pearl star and crescent pin for a visit to the ballet in Bath.

Left:
At a London charity evening in aid of Birthright in October 1987 the Princess of Wales chose an unusual dress in Elizabethan style with full cuffs and high ruffed collar by Catherine Walker. A heavy cross, lent by the jewellers, Wartski, on a long string of pearls was the finishing touch.

Remarkably this neat layered look has, even in its simplicity, been an attention-getter. Just a change in the way the Princess' hairdresser flicks the fringe, rolls and pins the back around a tiara, or changes a parting, draws comment from the insatiable press corps. From that point of view he has been extremely prolific. No one would have thought that the simple style she wore for her wedding day could have, or would have, been so versatile.

The wedding day hairdo was sadly one of the more low-key ideas, but it immediately linked the new Princess of Wales with her public in an unexpected yet strongly identifiable way. So many girls watching her that July day knew exactly what it was like to be let down by their hairdresser on the big day, even after regular salon rehearsals. However, Diana has gone on keeping it simple and, despite her glossy good looks, her hair has been the one aspect of her personal style that has constantly had a 'girl next door' appeal. Once her style had been established, variations on this Royal short-brushed hair cut appeared in all the hairdressing establishments and magazines. Young girls all over the country rushed to their local salons to have their hair cut like 'Lady Di' - an inaccurate title that she still has bestowed on her.

Elaborate ideas and hair ornaments are not often seen crowning the regal head of the Princess of Wales. In order to keep her elegant image she relies more on the elaborate lines of her dress and suit designs. She keeps accessories to a minimum and seems only to favour a hair ornament when there is a fashion, fun or diplomatic reason for it being used.

The Duchess of York, on the other hand, has both the self-confidence and the kind of hair that lends itself to all the latest wild hair ideas. This clearly alleviates her known boredom with simple fashion styling and gives everyone a great deal of pleasure.

One could say that having two young Royals with so many clever and diverse ideas on hair styling cannot be anything but good for the hairdressing industry, the already innovative hair ornament trade, or for anyone who wants to have a constant injection of creative hairdressing ideas. However, still the Princess and the Duchess suffer criticism for experimenting, something all young girls do. It invokes the most commonly used phrase about them and the other members of the Royal family -that 'they just can't win!'

Far left, top:
In April 1986, on a trip to Austria, the Princess had her longer layered look without so many 'highlights'. The necklace is a gem, the pendant of the Prince of Wales Feathers.

Far left, centre:
The Forties look according to Diana. The press went crazy for and against the Veronica Lake bob. It was given this stylish airing at a visit to a Deaf & Blind Rubella Centre in November 1984. Her suit was a great favourite, a hot pink wool crepe 'chauffeur' jacket by Jasper Conran.

Far left, bottom:
The 'Rocker' look that had the cameras following the Princess around and commenting on her new DA short cut and highlights.

Above:
Another of Catherine Walker's familiar designs worn by the Princess of Wales in Australia in 1988, this time without the large matching hat. Instead she wore designer sunglasses.

9 Style Setters

The British fashion industry is reputed to be turning over 50 billion pounds a year, and since 1981 owes more than a little of that success to its fashion leader—The Princess of Wales.

Ten years ago it would have been unthinkable to even contemplate that a member of the Royal family would be cast in this role and held responsible for creating most, if not all, of the latest fashion trends. But now it seems so commonplace that when, after Diana's success in this field, there was a new member of the Royal family, in the slightly different style of Sarah Ferguson, it is not surprising it should start all over again.

Not content with the willowy, model shape of our Princess of Wales, the fashion followers decided that the Duchess of York could also initiate trends. Whether, as with the Princess, she liked it or not! After all, they pointed out, she had borrowed clothes from the Princess so she couldn't be far off her size, and with her beautiful colouring she couldn't lose.

So after a few hurtful, pointedly critical, words, the Duchess abandoned her own style and pandered to theirs. And surprise, surprise!—once she adopted a few of the latest looks, not to mention a few well-chosen designers, she was fair game for the fashion world. She was launched on to the now-familiar guessing game of what was 'in' and what 'out'.

The whole merry-go-round of new ideas and trends dictates that the two young Royals have to get it right every time they step outside in something new. They have to be as regal as a Duchess and Princess but also fulfill the role of the girl-next-door, too. This impossible task, which has even been highlighted in a *Times* leader column, has meant that any outfit or accessory that appeals to the public might become an instant copy and, of course, make someone a fortune in the process.

Right:
Ascot 1987 and the Princess and Duchess enjoy a day at the races in the latest colour combination of navy and white. The Princess is in a striped silk outfit by Roland Klein and white straw Breton hat with navy band in petersham around the crown by Philip Somerville. The Duchess wears a white stubbed raw silk Cossack-style fitted jacket with navy trimmings and buttons. The skirt was the 'suitable' length on the knee in navy raw silk.

The spotted skirt and co-ordinating separates from Mondi, the German fashion house. The socks to match were an instant fashion craze. Stores sold out in two days of their appearance at polo in Windsor in 1986.

113

Right:
Demonstrating the art of feather-adorned fashion at an evening engagement at the Sadler's Wells Theatre in March 1987.

Below:
The big velvet bow that became another Sarah fashion winner, via Chanel, worn here at a visit to Duxford Air Museum in June 1986. Her collarless suit has a jade green jacket in viscose and linen, a white silk T-shirt and a very short black linen skirt, designed for her by Alistair Blair.

Right:
The Princess of Wales turning heads and making headlines in Australia in November 1985. Her gown in silk satin organza was studded all over with diamante and designed by Emanuel. The emerald and diamond choker belonged to Queen Mary, who left it to the Queen. She never wore it, so she gave it to the Princess of Wales who put it round her head!

Below:
The stunning coat from Arabella Pollen's collection in cream cashmere and wool trimmed in fake beaver, with some fur fabric used for a large floppy beret by Gilly Forge. Bella could have sold it 'over and over', it was such a success with customers. Its first appearance was during the tour of Germany in November 1987.

Top left:
The floral jeans that both the
Duchess and the Princess own
in several different prints. Sarah
has a blue pair that she bought
from Ralph Lauren and wore to
learn to fly. After she succeeded,
she declared them to be 'lucky'.

There are all sorts of double standards applied to Diana and Sarah now that they have become style setters. They have to be models, but not clothes horses. They have to be constantly desirable, but have minds of their own, and without making a single mistake or without a hint of rivalry they must be seen to be creating fashion, not following it.

This is, of course, abject nonsense. The reverse is most assuredly true. The puffball skirt was already part of the new decree from Paris when, being the diplomatic dresser she is, the Princess commissioned one from Catherine Walker and gave the Europeans a taste of Royal

Right:
Here the Duchess wears a
sophisticated black silk
camisole on a visit to Cardiff
in April 1987.

Above:
September 1986 and a visit to
Aycliffe School in County
Durham by the Duchess of York.
Stylish in black and white, she
rang the changes with this
suit, here with a 'teddy boy
bootlace tie'.

Left:
A coral faconne silk jaquard
suit by Jan Van Velden. One of
the three maternity outfits he
made for the Princess while she
was expecting Prince Henry.
The top had a bow under a
wing collar. The pleated skirt
had a full front made of pink
tucks and little side fastening
buttons. The hat in the same
fabric was by Freddie Fox.

Above:
The pleated skirt was taken in,
the top slimmed down, and the
Princess wears it very
successfully after the birth of her
second son Prince Henry.

high fashion. It should have been a seven-day wonder, but after the Royal endorsement we were stuck with some terrible sights on our high streets.

The Duchess of York's fitted bustle and peplum jackets were already features of a great many collections both in haute couture and ready-to-wear (their origin owed more to a certain Alexis Colby, a character in a highly-popular American 'soap', than to the Duchess of York).

However once several Royal designer suits had appeared, for example when Sarah accompanied her husband and the Queen on Her Majesty's 60th birthday to collect the thousands of daffodils from the singing children at Buckingham Palace, or the 'Polo mint' suit she

Another favourite that had a different adaptation two years later. The pretty silk dress and jacket by Catherine Walker had a simple gathered skirt in Australia, in April 1983, (above), and in Sicily (right) a pleated paralleled skirt and turned back hat, bringing it bang up to date.

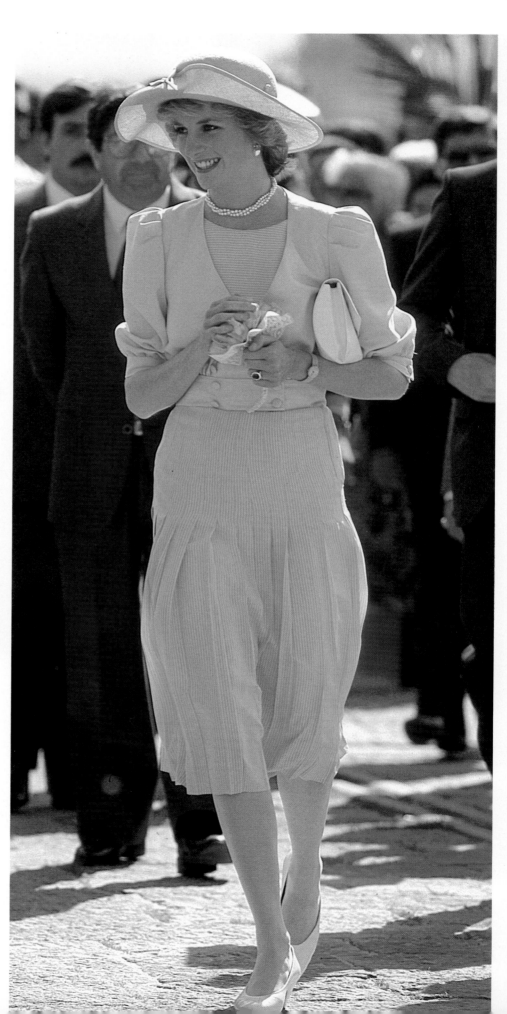

A favourite tartan suit worn year after year with different accessories. In November 1984 in Northamptonshire, her home county (top left), she wore it with blue satin shirt and matching tights. In February 1985 she went to Dr Barnardo's in Essex, (top centre) and wore it with a pink blouse and tights.
In Aberdeen in August 1986, (top right) she was seen with Prince William leaving the Royal Yacht Britannia with just the pink blouse and more subdued natural tights and navy shoes.

wore at Yellowknife, Canada, the peplum suit started to become part of occasion dressing for an eager-to-emulate British public.

It is said that imitation is the sincerest form of flattery, so the Duchess of York must have really understood the affection in which she is held when the famous black velvet bow burst upon the fashion scene. Large opulent bows, decorating full curling pony tails had always been a part of Karl Lagerfeld's repertoire, but when he produced them as part of the new Chanel look they were perfect. This winning feature of the German-born Parisian's collection for the classic fashion house was ideal for the Duchess's formal look and became an instant success with her followers. The fact that these accessories were part of an important couture statement from a leading fashion house was completely forgotten once the Duchess took to wearing them in a variety of fabrics and colours. These were 'Fergie Bows', and stores which made that point sold masses of them.

Their Royal Highnesses may be in a privileged position but to a certain extent they can never win in the fashion stakes.

Their following is not just with dyed-in-the-wool Royalists. They have another large group of admirers who watch them avidly for any fashionable endorsement and love to copy their looks.

If the Princess or the Duchess wears something with a strong fashion message, then for these followers it must be right. These girls have grown up watching and caring about the Princess of Wales since her magical marriage to Prince Charles, heir to the throne. Now they have a second fairytale to dream about, as the chosen bride of the handsome Prince Andrew is about to have her first Royal baby.

This fashion following probably wouldn't give a second glance to a report from the Paris collections. They only regard something as 'it', or 'hot', when the Princess, or any other of their idols, wears it. So it was with the spotted socks. The Princess appeared one weekend at

Right:
The Duke and Duchess of York attend the Royal Premiere of Slipstream *at the Odeon Cinema, Leicester Square, London. For the occasion she wore a full-skirted pink and black outfit.*

Above:
Pink, black and white make a bright outfit for the Duchess of York in October 1988.

Right:
October 1987. For the launch of 'One Day for Life' by Search 1988, at Claridges in London, the Duchess of York wore a pink dress with short grey jacket.

Far right, above:
Radcliffe Hospital, Oxford, 1986. With the candy striped blouse and with her Lady-in-Waiting, Anne Beckwith-Smith. This was the second visit to Oxford in the same suit. All clothes are logged according to where they were worn and with what, so this must have been a winner previously in Oxford!

Far right, below:
In a Victor Edelstein satin and lace two-piece with a scalloped hemline, the Princess of Wales attends a celebration of the 200th Anniversary of the founding of Australia in Sydney, January 1988.

Windsor in socks from a German co-ordinates manufacturer. They were bought from Harrods and were the nearest she was to get to looking like the girl next door. The shops sold out of anything remotely like a spotted sock within two days. Similarly, the floral collections that the top designers were successfully producing attracted both Diana and Sarah to Ralph Lauren's brand of softly printed pastel silks, cottons and, in particular, floral print jeans. The beauty of being a Royal is that when you really love a look, but cannot choose between the colours or the prints, you can actually have them all! Sarah's jeans from Ralph Lauren, in a bright blue print, were named 'lucky' after she wore them on her successful flying lessons. This spring you will see no other print as important to the high street shops, as floral, almost chintzy, prints.

It is undoubtedly true that just one appearance of a new fashion on either of these Royal figureheads will explode it into the high street, where it will be speedily sold.

There are, of course, exceptions to the rule. Diana has favoured scalloped hemlines, and worn necklaces in her hair. Sarah has

breathed new life into flying jackets and duchess satin. None of these has exactly saturated the high street as yet, despite the column inches claiming their importance to the current fashion scene at the time of their first Royal appearance.

Little touches made by the Royals to please their hosts and break the ice sometimes have nothing at all to do with fashion. The black bow tie on the Jasper Conran mandarin-collared suit worn by Diana on the Italian tour was simply a joke. Perhaps Jasper wouldn't have suggested it, but it *was* funny! Changing and adapting their clothes is something both the Princess and the Duchess do well in order to give a look a longer life or bring it up to date. Sarah is learning fast about that, with her formal suits given different blouses and ties, or new skirt silhouettes.

She will learn even more from her famous sister-in-law about ordering and adapting maternity outfits which can later be given a new life.

The Princess became something of an expert in this difficult fashion problem when expecting Prince Henry, and turned to designer Jan Van Velden.

Many of her more chic maternity outfits during her first pregnancy with Prince William were exactly that—maternity outfits. Although she enjoyed wearing them, she did not like the waste, so with her second son on the way she made sure that some of her maternity clothes had a longer life. Jan made oufits which, after the birth, could look just as chic. On one particular coral silk outfit he spent hours of work, painstakingly pin-tucking the front of the skirt and making the fastening adjustable with buttoned sides.

The Princess found it so comfortable in pregnancy that it became a favourite which she wore on some very important occasions, with an elegant matching hat.

Her ability to make her favourite outfits work for her is a clear sign of her real fashion intelligence.

Any of her followers wanting to imitate real style could do no better than study the way she takes an ordinary suit and makes it

The perfect compliment to the Japanese, the red rising sun on white background fabric that matches the Japanese national flag. The Princess was on a tour of Japan, in May 1986.

125

look easy, elegant, or city smart just with a simple change of hat, a different shade of tights, or a blouse.

It takes confidence, but with the adoration she has gained over the years this is no longer a problem. Boldness may not yet be her strength, but she has overcome her shyness.

It also takes organisation and here we can all learn from her unique way of 'filing' fashion. With the help of her dresser, Evelyn Dagley, the Princess has a system within her large dressing room, off the enormous main bedroom in Kensington Palace. Everything there is arranged according to colour, hanging in its own protective cover. Even the accessories, shoes and belts, are kept in their own cupboards and stored by colour.

Keeping everything neatly together in this way makes it easy to see whether there is a need for a new outfit. If so, it is quickly apparent how best it can be utilised and just what accessories are needed, if any are needed at all. The system enables Her Royal Highness to plan ahead without having to memorise every detail. It is the responsibility of the dresser to log the details of when each item is worn and with which accessories. It is her job, too, to provide the details of the outfit released to the press during the Royal Tour. As colour is so important, a simple browse establishes any shortcomings the Royal wardrobe might have.

The use of colour to its best effect is something that the Royal Family has always practised. They always find a truly startling colour, without brashness, to make sure they can be picked out in a crowd and seen more easily.

Their Royal Highnesses continue this tradition, but also go one step further—they like to use colour to indicate their delight at the visit or tour. For example on a tour in 1986 to Japan the Princess wore not only the colours of the Japanese flag but also its symbol—a red sun on a white background.

It worked as both an attention-getter and a simply splendid way of showing warmth between one country and another.

Sarah doing the same—complimenting the Canadians with her red and white outfit and 'Maple Leaf' hat by Graham Smith. He suggested it as he devised this bow back style to thread her hair through. She thought, 'They'll love it!'. She was right.

Doing it again . . . this time the national flower of Mauritius tucked under her hat. The hat is by Siggi and the outfit by David Sassoon of Bellville Sassoon.

Visiting the Red Arrows in May 1987, with darts in the double bow to honour the team.

Above:
The Princess of Wales seems to be measuring the ribbon on her bouquet as she arrives at the Brooklyn Academy of Music in New York to hear the Welsh National Opera's Gala production of Verdi's Falstaff, followed by dinner at the Wintergarden.

Above:
The Duchess of York in a floral dress visiting the Nordoff Music Therapy Centre, Kentish Town in March 1989. While staying at Holyrood House, Edinburgh, she wore the same dress with navy jacket and gold buttons.